RECOVER *LIFE*
Instead of
SPENDING *LIFE*
Recovering

Dealing with the Loss of a Loved One

B . J . T H O M P S O N

ISBN 978-1-63961-770-8 (paperback)
ISBN 978-1-63961-771-5 (digital)

Christian Faith Publishing, Inc.
832 Park Avenue
Meadville, PA 16335
www.christianfaithpublishing.com

Printed in the United States of America

CONTENTS

CHAPTER **1**

WHAT HAPPENED TO ME?

(Confusion, Fear, and Hurt)

My wife, Joyce, and I had driven about one hour to be at an "away" high school volleyball game that our two granddaughters were playing in. It was late afternoon, around five o'clock, and the contest was nearing its end. We were looking forward to meeting with Kayla and Ashley, telling them they played well, and stopping at some restaurant before we drove home.

Joyce looked at me with surprise and said, "I can't move my left leg." There were no symptoms, no previous warnings; what could possibly be wrong? Then she said, "I can't move my right leg either." Oh, she looked so surprised and scared.

I felt so helpless. She had never had any problems like this before! I did not have my cell phone to call for emergency help; but fortunately, someone else called. Emergency arrived fairly quickly. They took her to the emergency room at a nearby hospital. I followed in our car alone. You can imagine all the thoughts that went through my head and the questions there were in my confusion and fear about what had happened.

Something had happened to my high school sweetheart, married for fifty-one years, and I could not do anything about it.

It was God's providence that the volleyball game was away, and we were in Lakewood, Ohio. The Cleveland Clinic had a hospital within three miles that had a unit that specialized in brain trauma. Joyce received the best possible care and best possible chance to live that she could have had. Thank you, Lord, for that peace!

I did not get to be apprised of her condition or be with her for about five hours. In that time, she had been taken from the emergency room and moved to the intensive care unit of their department specializing in the brain. When I finally got to be with Joyce, she was hooked up to many tubes and devices and was nonresponsive. I could only just sit there and pray.

In the meantime, I had found a phone and had called our four children and told them what happened. It was late at night, but they started showing up.

The doctor finally appeared and told me that there was no specific diagnosis as to what had happened to Joyce, and they were continuing to test to find out. They did not know how long that would take. Well, there was no way that I was not going to stay all night and as many nights as it took to have her back. So I camped in their waiting room, waiting for her diagnosis and treatment.

The waiting room was large with the capacity, I would estimate, of twenty-five people. It had three couches you could sleep on. So I, and a few others, slept there each night for twenty-four days, waiting and hoping for some good news. During the day, the waiting room was full of family and friends who had come to support us. After a few nights, the hospital gave us a room that three people could sleep in, and they also supplied the waiting room with a refrigerator for our use.

Joyce's condition remained the same for about five days. The doctors had hoped that there was no damage, and she could heal. However, on the sixth day, the doctors said that her brain was swelling, and they had to remove a portion of her skull to give her brain room to swell. So we, the family, agreed to the operation.

The operation was a success, and there was a hope that the swelling would end and then go down to normal. We were encouraged and had new hope that all the different tests and treatments that they were doing were going to bring her back to normal.

With all the tests they were doing, they still could not determine how much damage had been done. At one time, the doctor said there may be damage, and Joyce could lose the use of one side of her body. Hey! I would take that if I can just have her back. There was still hope.

But six days later, Joyce had to have another brain operation because her brain started swelling again.

I tried to be in Joyce's room as much as I could throughout her whole hospital stay. When I was not there, we always made sure at least one person was in the room with her, reading to her, praying, or just being there.

Two weeks passed, and we did not have any diagnosis, but we still had hope that there was no damage. Then three weeks passed, and we still had hope. We were doing everything we could—being there, praying in her room, and in the waiting room, encouraging the doctor—to get our Joyce back.

In the fourth week and two operations later, the doctor told us that there was irreparable damage, and there was nothing that could be done. We were crushed; all hope was gone. There was not going to be a wife, a mother, a grandmother, a great-grandmother, a sister, and a best friend.

She was a woman of God. She loved her heavenly Father, read the Bible, and prayed her prayer list every morning. Why did God take her in such a hurtful way? There was no chance to tell her how much we loved her and what a wonderful impact she had had on so many lives, no chance to thank her for her love and support, no chance to pray with her, knowing that she was going to die. Most hurtful of all, there was no chance for any words of goodbye for me, her four children, nine grandchildren, and four great-grandchildren. There was much we all wanted to do and say, but there was nothing but silence.

Thirty days and most nights in the intensive care unit room, with all the confusion and unknowns, I was exhausted.

Then the viewing, funeral service, and burial—I went home alone. It was over. So now what happens?

I do not remember much about the next six months except I remember my faith in God was sorely tested. I had many questions for God. I had many questions about what I should believe about my confusion, fear, and hurt and how I should act as a Christian. I also realized that I was not prepared for Joyce's death; and I did not know what was going to happen to my future life after one-half of my being was not there anymore.

CHAPTER 2

I SOUGHT HELP

What do I do now? Where do I go to get help?

With my loss, amid the various emotions, confusion, fear, and hurt I was experiencing, I looked for information and direction on how to deal with my grief and heal.

I started by reading over thirty books about losing a loved one. I found they varied in content and approach with some helpful information. In addition, I attended my church's grief program and two other separate grief programs, one faith based, and the other nonfaith based. I was reading, listening to teachings, watching videos, and filling out workbooks that told me what was going to happen to me and what I needed to understand and to do to heal. As a whole, I learned many important things I needed to know. I am thankful for each author and teacher for the time and effort that they put forth to try to help me, a survivor. But I did not feel that any one of those sources contained all of the information needed for a survivor to heal and lead the meaningful and fulfilled life that I wished for myself and the meaningful and fulfilled life I wished for other survivors.

Consequently, I have taken all the valuable information I have learned from many books and other literature regarding grief, then added the practical aspects of grief I have learned from creating a new grief program, **Grieving with Hope**, and leading, and interacting with survivors in that program several times. I believe that the combination of information in this book provides everything any survivor needs to know to heal, recover life, and lead a meaningful and fulfilled life. This book should help every survivor who reads it no matter their circumstances. You may find parts of this book do not apply to you; but I assure you, there are parts that will help you! Hang in there, and keep reading!

I was faced with the dilemma of what information should I supply to you when you and every other person who reads this book is unique and completely different from each other. (Your uniqueness will be developed later.) So how do I write a meaningful book when each reader is uniquely different and will react differently to the information provided, depending on their individual circumstances and needs? My answer: Put everything in this book that could be helpful, and let each reader find what is helpful to them.

Be aware that any general comments I make regarding grief and healing are made to the readers who are most seriously affected (loss of spouse, child, parent, sibling, best friend), but the subject matter will be helpful no matter how seemingly controllable or manageable your situation seems to be or how severely out of control and unsolvable your situation seems to be.

CHAPTER **3**

THE GOALS OF THIS BOOK

(This Is What You Need to Know!)

God has provided me with the answers for your healing. I want your healing to be complete and to result in the following:

Goal 1—your understanding of **how the process of grief works**. Your understanding will help you deal with the emotional turmoil you are experiencing (i.e., eliminating the confusion, fear, and hurt).

Goal 2—your having recovered and **having a new life that is meaningful and fulfilled. If your new life takes on meaning and becomes fulfilled**, then it will result in giving you hope and a peace in your new life.

Goal 3—your walking away from this book, feeling that **you are loved**; that you are **able to heal and recover your new life** because you are a special person; that you are **worthy of recognition and to be cared about**; and that **protection (security), understanding, strengthening, and purpose are available in your new life** if only you will just accept it.

Goal 1 (to heal) and Goal 2 (recovering a meaningful and fulfilled new life) are what a survivor wants to understand and experience as quickly as possible to get rid of the confusion, fear, and hurt so they can feel secure in their new life. So why is Goal 3 important to a survivor? The reason is that unless a survivor obtains the results in Goal 3 above, they probably will never deal with Goals 1 and 2 effectively and end up just spending life recovering and never finally fully recover their life. Why do I say that? Because there is a natural tendency for a survivor to feel confusion and fear and slowly start to lose confidence in themselves, just when they need to believe in themselves and their ability the most. Why wouldn't that happen? Here are some of the hurtful and damaging feelings a survivor is experiencing:

- They become isolated and lonely.
- They are feeling unsupported and abandoned by family and friends.
- They feel unprotected and afraid.
- They are experiencing a lot of confusion and new challenges and starting to wonder if they are able to handle things.
- Doubt starts a survivor thinking they are unworthy, unloved, or not cared about.

Thus, the third goal is necessary to reinforce the confidence a survivor needs to have in themselves (that they are loved and worthy, they are cared about, they are able, they are protected and strengthened), so the major discouragements and hurtful things confronting a survivor do not keep the survivor from ever confronting and trying to accomplish goals 1 and 2.

The above three goals are important for a survivor to understand and know that no matter how bad a survivor feels or whatever insurmountable situation they seem to be in that they are loved and cared about, that they are capable to handle the confusion and messy situation they have been put in, that there is hope. Then they will be able to get through their grief and recover to have a new **meaningful and fulfilled life**.

Goal 4—is to help the survivor travel the spiritual journey they need to reaffirm their faith in God by coming to understanding about what the Bible says about their loss and the Bible's answers to their many spiritual questions. Having those answers allows a survivor to make more sense of their Christian walk and helps them to persevere and end up with a meaningful and fulfilled life.

PUTTING DEATH IN PERSPECTIVE AND UNDERSTANDING GRIEF—WHAT IS GRIEF?

Here are some comments about death that show its severity and confirms the intensity of your feelings and situation:

- Death rips a hole in our understanding of **the meaning of life**.
- Death confronts us with "you are not in **control of your life**." (It is not difficult to see how this threatens your security.)
- Death tears at the fabric of your being and requires changes in your life to accommodate the realities of your new life.
- Bereavement is the deepest initiation into the mysteries of human life, an initiation more searching and profound than even happy love (Dean Inge).
- Death leaves one **with a choice: live in the past** (stay in the tattered space of our life, clutching at the torn

remnants of our past, mourning the empty spaces, and breathing the stagnant air), or **look to the future** (find a unique and new mission in life and a new reason to face life).

• Death leaves you with a choice: it can lead you to an abyss, or you can build a bridge that will span the caverns.

Grief is not just one thing; it is the whole healing process one goes through to heal and then start living a meaningful and fulfilled new life.

Some observations on grief:

No one ever told me that grief felt so like fear. I am not afraid, but the sensation is like being afraid. The same fluttering in the stomach, the same restlessness, the yawning. I keep on swallowing. At other times, it feels like being mildly drunk, or concussed. There is a sort of an **invisible blanket between the world and me**. I find it hard to take in what anyone says. Or perhaps, hard to want to take it in. It is so uninteresting. Yet I want the others to be about me. I dread the moments when the house is empty. If only they would talk to one another and not to me. There are moments, most unexpectedly, when something inside me tries to reassure me that I do not really mind so much, not so very much, after all. Love is not the whole of man's life. I was happy before I ever met (my loved one). I've plenty of what are called "resources". People get over these things. Come, I shan't do so badly. One is ashamed to listen to this voice, but it seems, for a little, to be making a good case. Then comes a sudden jab of red-hot memory, and all this "commonsense" vanishes like an ant in the mouth of a furnace. (**C. S. Lewis,** *A Grief Observed*)

Grief changes us. The pain sculpts us into someone who: understands more deeply, hurts more often, appreciates more quickly, cries more easily, hopes more desperately, and loves more often. (**Anonymous**)

Grief is a process of awareness, of making real inside the self an event that already occurred in reality outside. (**Parkes & Weiss**)

Grief is a tidal wave that overtakes you, smashes down upon you with unimaginable force, sweeps you up into its darkness where you tumble and crash against unidentifiable surfaces only to be thrown out on an unknown beach, bruised, reshaped... Grief will make a new person out of you if it doesn't kill you in the making. (**Stephanie Ericsson**)

Grief, I've learned, is really just love. It is all the love you want to give but cannot. All that unspent love gathers up in the corners of your eyes, the lump in your throat, and that hollow part of our chest. Grief is just love with no place to go. (**Jamie Anderson**)

I must tell you that I started out on my walk with grief with a total misconception of how grief worked. I thought grief was just another major aspect of life that one experiences where you learn about it, find out how to deal with it, and it would ultimately go away.

But everything I studied kept saying, **"Grief will never leave you**. It will always be there in your life until the end."

I then realized that grief is not a wound or a sickness where a procedure or medicine or therapy will cure it, and one is healed, and the experience is over.

Grief will never go away because it is a part of you. It is part of you because of who you were (when in your loving relationship) and who you are today (who you have been molded into because of that loving relationship). So it becomes a part of you and a personal memory never to be forgotten.

> The reality is that you will grieve forever. You will not "get over" the loss of a loved one. You will learn to live with it. You will heal, and you will rebuild yourself around the loss you have suffered. You will be whole again, but you will never be the same nor would you want to. **(Dr. Elisabeth Kubler-Ross)**

> Grief never ends, but it changes. It is a passage, not a place to stay. Grief is the price of a love lost.
>
> From a survivor, I assumed that every day would get better and easier. That does not happen! Grief is a roller coaster of ups and downs. BE AWARE, there is not a typical response to loss as there is not a typical loss.

GRIEF

I had my own notion of grief.
I thought it was a sad time
That followed the death of someone you love.
And you had to push through it
To get to the other side.
But I am learning there is no other side.

17

There is no pushing through
But rather
There is Absorption
Adjustment
Acceptance
And grief is not something you complete
But rather that you endure.
Grief is not a task to finish
And move on
But an element of yourself
An alteration of your being
A new way of seeing
A new delineation of self.(**Barb Mather**)

What does the grief process look like?

Losing a loved one creates a future life with two parts a survivor must deal with.

In her book, *Bearing the Unbearable: Love, Loss, and the Heartbreaking Path of Grief,* Joanne Cacciatore, PhD, believes a survivor has the strength to have a life with cohabitants in it:

- A **NEW LIFE** of finding out what is going to happen to the survivor in the future, new challenges of finding out who they really are and what their purpose is in life.
- **A process of grief** that deals with the emotions and various crises that arise because of the **memories the survivor wants to acknowledge and keep about** the past part of their life they **spent with their lost loved one**.

She warns there is a tendency for the survivor to rush into their **NEW LIFE** activities and minimize or eliminate their desire (in fact need) to retain memories of their past life with their loved one.

Two major reasons for this mistake (rushing into their **NEW LIFE**) are as follows:

- It's easier **to avoid** the confusion, fear, and hurt of grief by not confronting grief.
- The survivor's **environment** is uncomfortable with the grief process and encourages as quick of a closure as possible.

The above minimizing or elimination of the grief process ignores the special significance of the loved one's loss to the survivor and should not happen—significant because the time spent with the lost loved one that the survivor wants to forever remember was a time of love. That time of love is a part of the survivor and should not be expected to be discarded and forgotten.

The above is why there is no end to the grief process. It will never be forgotten or go away because it is part of one's life in the past based on **love**.

Intense confusion, fear, and hurt are felt at the beginning, but as the years go by, the painful part will temper, and the survivor will be more at peace with the memories they kept.

Unfortunately, a very important step in healing, **feeling your feelings** and their expression is repressed by society (described elsewhere). The survivor's own fear of upsetting or affecting listeners in a negative way also represses expression, thus, the needed expression of their feelings is very difficult, if not impossible.

Unfair as the above is, a survivor must find someone who cares, not just cares a little. They must enter into the confusion, fear, and hurt of the survivor to the point of feeling what the survivor feels and pledge to spend their time and energy sacrificially—a herculean task but the most effective support.

From my observations, the grief process involves the following areas you must be aware of and deal with: (I have listed these crises in a sequence that most survivors experience.)

- An **EMOTIONAL CRISIS**: How do you deal with the many and varied emotions in different intensities at different times? You are thinking weird things and acting differently. Is something wrong with you? Are you going crazy?

Most likely, you will experience the emotions of shock, at first, then denial (that this tragedy has happened), to confusion, to fear, to anger, and on through the various emotions you will experience. You will work through those emotions toward your final goal of accepting your loss and adjusting to be at peace with your loss and your future new life. Emotions are hard to deal with. Like waves in the ocean, they swell-up and then recede, they disappear, and then reappear, always changing and reacting to what is happening in your future new life.

To heal, you must do two things about your emotional crisis:

- Learn everything you can about the different emotions you are going to experience, understand them, and learn how to deal with them.
- Start to talk about whatever is happening in your situation (your sadness, loneliness, your concerns, your confusion, etc.) outwardly to whomever you trust as much as possible.

Emotions must be dealt with first because until you have adjusted emotionally, your emotions put you in a state of not wanting to hear or not being able to hear the rest of the things you need to know to heal.

- A **CAPABILITY CRISIS**: You wonder if you will be able to handle this mess that has just been handed to you? There is so much you do not understand!

Right away, you must deal with the unwanted, everyday living problems that arise in continuing to live while in the grief process (financial condition, family problems, friends' problems, job problems, car problems, etc.). Your probable response is **"Why was I left with this mess? I have become totally responsible for everything even though I do not understand some or all parts of it."** Of course there is great confusion here and justifiably so! You did not expect this to happen, and you had not received any formal preparation for it.

A survivor is going to have to deal with their EMOTIONAL and CAPABILITY CRISES **right away.**

- A **CHARACTER CRISIS**: Who am I? **Do I have the strength and character** to heal and have a **meaningful and fulfilled new life**? Or am I going to be left floundering here?

As a survivor struggles through the grief process with all its unknowns and questions, they are confronted with periods of time when they start to **have questions and doubts about who they are, their own identity (Who am I?), and their worthiness (Do they have any importance or significance in life or any contribution to make to their new life?).** Because of these unknowns, I have observed that they start to lose confidence in themselves, they start doubting their thinking and actions and start questioning what qualities they really have.

This dilemma can be devastating because **right at the time when a survivor needs the most confidence, support, and encouragement, all those attributes are waning.**

- An **EXPECTATION CRISIS**: why aren't things working out as you expected they would? There are so many surprises and disappointments! What should you expect to happen realistically, so you are not hurt so much?

A survivor's expectations as to what is going to happen in their healing process are usually unrealistic and over optimistic. There is nothing wrong with that because they were not prepared for their loss and do not know what to expect will happen. However, **the higher the expectations the bigger the disappointments, hurt and confusion** when they are not met; thus, adding to the confusion, fear, and hurt they are already experiencing. Therefore, a survivor needs to be educated about what realistically is going to happen to them and learn from those who have experienced grief so that their expectations can be adjusted to what is most likely, realistically to happen.

- A **SPIRITUAL CRISIS**: Are you going to try to heal alone without God or with God?

Where does one go to for counsel, understanding, and healing when they have lost a loved one?

One alternative is to go to family, friends, counselors (experts?), or others who have a worldly view. The other alternative is to depend on God and His Word, fellowship with His children, and His everlasting love for the survivor. **God's Word provides hope and peace.**

- The **"WHY" QUESTION CRISIS**: How can you make any sense out of all this confusion, fear, and hurt so you can have peace and understanding about it, start your healing, and move on?

An uneasy feeling that underlies the grief healing process is the **"WHY"** questions.

Why did this happen to me? Did somebody do something wrong? **Why did a loving God let** this happen? etc. Answers to these questions are needed to help a survivor **make as much sense** of what happened as possible. The more answers to the **"WHY"** questions, the more meaning and purpose there is in what happened, and the more sense and ensuing acceptance, **HEALING**, and moving on by the survivor.

- The **WHAT IS MY VALUE? WHAT IS MY PURPOSE IN LIFE NOW?** CRISIS: As healing progresses and the survivor is dealing better with their new life, they are confronted with the exceedingly difficult question of **what their purpose in life is**, and, if not evident, how do **they determine what that purpose is**?

A life without purpose just becomes bearable/ livable and will not develop into a meaningful and purpose-filled life.

- The **WHAT DO I DO TO HEAL NOW?** CRISIS: Initially, a survivor is not in an emotional state to want to hear all they need to hear, but in time, they will need to learn what steps to take to heal the most effectively. Thinking (the right thoughts) and doing the right activities can substantially reduce the intensity of the confusion, fear, and hurt they will experience and substantially reduce the time it takes to heal. The specific steps a survivor needs to take are provided later.

Be aware, no survivor is going to escape going through the grief process. Even if a survivor already understood everything about the grief process and had all the answers to healing and regaining a meaningful and fulfilled life, they are going to experience the emotions caused by the loss of a loved one. Why? Just because they are human. Emotions are built in, and they are going to come no matter what. They must be expected, recognized, and dealt with.

CHAPTER 5

GRIEF IS UNHEALTHY AND DANGEROUS

(A Survivor Needs to Get Serious about the
Importance of Healing and Doing It Right!)

There are approximately eight hundred thousand new widows
and widowers each year (National Mental Health Association).

Psychiatric News stated that 40 percent of survivors are in
depression one month after the loss of a loved one and 24 percent remain in depression after two months, and 10–15 percent
are in a depression for longer periods of time.

Remy Melina (January 13, 2012, Live Science) found that
in the

- first twenty-four hours after the death of a loved one,
  risk of a heart attack is twenty-one times greater;
- first week after the death of a loved one, risk of heart
  attack is eight time greater.

A University of Michigan Retirement and Health study of
12,316 participants who became married and were then followed for ten years (1998–2008), concluded that a survivor

who had lost a spouse in this group had a 66 percent increased chance of dying within the first three months of their loved one's death. Then the increased likelihood of dying reduced to 15 percent after three months. ("How the 'Widowhood Effect' Puts Widows at Risk After a Spouse's Death," Harvard School of Public Health—Dr. S. V. Subramanian, https://www.verywell-mind.com/surviving widowhood-0411236)

WebMD's survey of 780 people who had experienced a grief event in the past three years, from May 2016 through May 2019, resulted in the following statistics about a survivor's condition after the loss of a spouse:

- Forty-eight percent said their most powerful feelings subsided within six months, and 67 percent felt they had recovered within one year.
- Fifty-eight percent of survivors who were "pressured to heal too quickly" felt they were expected by others to recover within three months.
- Ninety-one percent felt they were expected to move on within one year.

TIME NEEDED TO GRIEVE

Approximately how long was the most intense part of your grieving for the incident?	Death of a loved one*	Death of a pet	Serious illness	Friendship/relationship
Less than six months	48%	66%	40%	45%
Less than twelve months	68%	81%	58%	65%
More than one year	12%	7%	13%	20%
I am still intensely grieving	18%	12%	24%	15%

(* death of a child, spouse/partner, family member, or close friend.)

A. Eighty-eight percent had some type of emotional symptom and 68 percent had physical symptoms (for example: 59 percent fatigue and 48 percent change of appetite).
B. Fifty-three percent of survivors dealt with their grief by spending more time with other people.
C. Thirty-one percent were more likely to turn to religion or spiritual practices.
D. To me, the most concerning statistic is that only 5 percent attended in-person or online support groups/discussion forums, and only 6 percent used professional counseling.

Judging from my own experience in terms of what needs to be done to heal, I would have to question whether many of these survivors who thought they were healed really ended up totally healed with purposeful and fulfilled lives! Consequently, I think the above time lines to heal are skewed, and recovery takes a lot longer than shown.

That is why I am writing this book! LET'S GET IT RIGHT!
WebMD's study also provided some other helpful statistics about survivors.

- Sixty-six percent said someone tried to cheer them up. (Fifty-four percent said it worked; 36 percent felt it was ineffective.)
- Seventy-four percent of survivors had someone share their own person experience with loss with them. (Fifty-three percent said it helped; 37 percent felt it was ineffective.)

ALSO, SURVIVORS HAD THE FOLLOWING ADVICE OFFERED:

- "It could be worse." (Sixteen percent felt it was effective; 46 percent felt worse afterward.)

- "Move on or seek closure as soon as possible." (16 percent felt it was effective; 42 percent felt worse afterward.)
- Various unsolicited advices (Nineteen percent felt it was effective; 33 percent felt worse afterward.) ("Grief Beyond the 5 Stages", July 11, 2019, https://www.WEBMD.com/special-reports/Grief-Stages/20190711/The-Grief-Experience-Survey-Shows-Its-complicated)

A mental health clinical team's research concluded that the symptoms of complicated grief in the bereaved elderly were cancer, hypertension, anxiety, depression, suicidal ideation, increased smoking, and sleep impairment at around six months after a spousal death. (Rasenzweig, MD; Prigerson, PhD; Miller, MD; Reynolds Lii, MD 1997. "Bereavement and Late-Life Depression: Grief and Its complications in the Elderly." Annual Review of Medicine 48:421-8.doi:10-1146/Annurev.med.48.1.421.PMID 9046973)

After a major loss, such as death of a spouse or child, up to a third of the people most directly affected will suffer detrimental effects on their physical or mental health or both. Such bereavements increase the risk of death from heart disease and suicide as well as causing or contributing to a variety of psychosomatic and psychiatric disorders. About a quarter of widows and widowers will experience clinical depression and anxiety during the first year of bereavement; the risk drops to about 17 percent by the end of the first year and continues to decline thereafter. They found that 31 percent of seventy-one patients admitted to a psychiatric unit for the elderly had recently been bereaved. ("Bereavement in Adult Life," The bmj-1998 Mar 14, Colin Murray Parkes, Consultant Psychiatrist https://www.ncbi.nim.nih.gov/pmc/articles/PMC1112778)

Despite the above, there is also evidence that losses can foster maturity and personal growth. Losses are not necessarily harmful; but neglecting to take the needed steps to heal will be harmful.

CHAPTER **6**

RESULTS OF YOUR PRESENT SITUATION— CONFUSION, FEAR, HURT

(How Are You Feeling?)

Let's face it, the loss of your loved one has turned your world upside down. You do not even want to admit that your situation is as bad as it is. There is an underlying feeling that there is so much confusion, fear, and hurt that you may never be able to heal and recover back to a normal life.

Throughout this book, I am going to refer to your condition as **confusion**, **fear**, and **hurt**.

CONFUSION because virtually, everything has changed. People do not even like small changes in their life, and this all-encompassing change is devastating. Do not feel lost and incompetent because you are having trouble dealing with your confusion, **so are the other survivors**.

FEAR—I will use the word **fear** because it is the most subtle of the things you are dealing with. In fact, most survivors are not even aware that they are subconsciously feeling a lot of fear. Everything has changed, everything is coming up different, and there is an underlying feeling that you cannot handle it all, and you are going to fail and hurt even more.

HURT—I use the word **hurt**, instead of pain, because I believe pain is just something you feel physically. Pain comes and goes eventually with physical healing. However, hurt is a lingering mental feeling of not knowing what is going to happen, whether your various hurts are ever going to heal and the seemingly unfairness of your situation.

So in your confusion, fear, and hurt, this book offers you what you need to be aware of in grief and the steps you need to take to heal. Healing is the **first part** of your journey and consists of learning about

- the things you need to know about the grief process and the various crises you will face;
- the activities you need to do starting today, if possible, or when you are able to begin healing and recover life instead of spending your life recovering.

The **second part** of your healing is to make sure your new life does not end up just being bearable and livable. Rather, you can be at peace with the loss of your loved one and experience a meaningful and fulfilled new life.

Your goal is (little steps at a time) to learn, listen, take the actions recommended (as soon as you are able), be nice to yourself, and remember you are worthy, capable, loved, and special in God's eyes (even though you may not feel that way right now).

THE UNSETTLING EFFECTS OF GRIEF

WHAT A SURVIVOR HAS LOST IS SUBSTANTIAL.

You, the survivor, have experienced much more loss than you know, and you will be confronted with unexpected losses and disappoints in the future. Don't worry. Life experiences will remind you of how much you have lost. I experienced it as **life slaps you in the face** with another loss or disappointment.

What have you lost?

- **COMPANIONSHIP OF YOUR LOVED ONE**—Who gave you love, caring, acceptance, worthiness, and sharing? Loneliness is one of the most crushing experiences.
- **DIRECTION**—Guidance, sharing of thinking, desires, wants, needs, and goals
- **SAFETY**—You have lost your protection.
- **SOCIAL ACTIVITIES**—Meetings and other activities with friends and social groups become more restricted.
- **MOBILITY**—Becoming limited, especially in the evening.

So in the midst of the devastating changes and losses mentioned above and the resulting emotions, it makes it exceedingly difficult to apply yourself to your everyday living needs and requirements and to properly relate to others. No wonder you are confused and questioning many things and confronted with doubts about whether you can or are handling things properly.

Hey! Despite all the above, you are okay where you are right now. Death and the resulting grief are so unfair. You were not prepared for it, and it resulted in many more unanticipated changes and losses in your life than you expected. All the confusion is understandable. It is not a result or sign of your weakness or your inability to handle your situation.

Do not lose faith.

Do not feel unable or incapable of working through the healing process.

You can do it.

You are in the same confusing position that most, if not all, survivors start in not because you did something wrong or cannot handle it, but there are valid reasons why your present situation is so confusing.

Remember, you are okay where you are right now!

THE AMOUNT OF CHANGE IS UNDERESTIMATED.

When a loved one dies, the average person pretty much understands some things are going to change. But one thinks that life, as a survivor, will go on pretty much as it did because there is the same home, family, community, friends, etc. But that expectation is totally wrong. When you think about it, **virtually, everything has changed**!

You are not prepared for the amount of emotions and everyday problems you will experience. Survivors far underestimate the amount of change, confusion, and disappointments that will happen in their life.

How much change is there? Recognize that after your loss, virtually, everything you do is different because your loved one is no longer a part of your life and decision-making. Not just a little change, **everything has changed**!

Do not feel inadequate or unable to handle your situation. You must recognize the severity of the change in your life (i.e., Every thought, every activity, every decision is different since your loss. Your loved one is no longer involved.) No wonder there is confusion, even fear, trying to deal with the volume and severity of the unexpected changes.

TIME CONSIDERATIONS

You will find that time is not your friend as it seems like your healing takes too long. You do not know how long to expect for healing to take. You will find that others will be happy to give you their opinion on timing even though they are different from you, and they have not experienced what you are experiencing.

You may not be allowed the time to heal because of your circumstances. If you are in a position where you have very little time for yourself to heal because you are forced to work or provide care for someone else, you will not have the time nor energy to take the steps you need to take to heal.

Do not fall into a trap. Do not let life demands make you so busy you cannot take some time to start your healing. You must! Analyze where your time is being spent. Be good to yourself, and just say "no" to the least important activities. You need to dedicate some time and energy to help yourself by learning about the grief healing process and what you need to understand.

CHAPTER 8

THINGS YOU MUST KNOW ABOUT THE GRIEF PROCESS YOU MAY HAVE NOT THOUGHT ABOUT

(The Melting Pot of Grief)

There are major aspects of grief that a survivor does not know about until they have lost a loved one and start experiencing them. Being aware of the following is extremely helpful in the healing process.

YOUR UNIQUENESS IS IMPORTANT.

This is something that is basic that you need to keep reminding yourself of through your grief process. You are unique. You are like a fingerprint or a snowflake **with no match**.

You, and every other person who has suffered the loss of a loved one, are **COMPLETELY DIFFERENT FROM EACH OTHER**.

Why? Because each person's past physical, mental, and spiritual experiences combine to make them different in their life experiences and unique in their reactions to a loss.

Because you are so unique, you must realize that whatever state you are in right now, emotionally, expectation-wise, physically, spiritual, etc., **you are okay right where you are**.

You are okay even though **emotionally** you are all over the place. You are angry then sad with tears then sometimes quietly depressed then fearful. Different emotions seem to pop-up with the different situations you experience. You are wondering if you can hold this painful experience together and not fall apart. You sometimes question your actions because they seem to be **abnormal**. But what you need to know is that your **abnormal thoughts and actions are normal** at the start of your healing.

After the completion of my grief programs, several of the participants commented that the most valuable thing they learned was **that they were okay right where they were, mentally and physically**, at the beginning. They were afraid that their thoughts and actions were so exaggerated that there was something wrong with them, even thoughts they might be going crazy!

I want to encourage you that you are capable, and you can heal and work your way back to a meaningful and fulfilled life. The confusion, fear, and hurt you are feeling are not a sign of your being weak, inadequate, or unable to handle your situation. You are normal and must understand that most survivors are going through the same crippling and disabling experiences you are experiencing. You were made that way. It is just natural!

You are okay because society is not geared to prepare a survivor for the death of a loved one.

It seems like no one wants to talk about death. How could you possibly be prepared for it?

As an example, in my forty years of practice as an estate planner, it was exceedingly difficult to get my clients to do any preliminary planning for death, even the simplest steps as making sure one had a simple will or an estate plan. The reality is that most people do not like to think about themselves dying, or in fact, others dying. They do not even want to learn about what happens at death, or about what needs to be done before death happens.

If the people who are most directly affected by death (terminally Ill people or their loved ones or caretakers) do not take action to prepare for when death comes, who then is there to help prepare a survivor for the death of a loved one?

So the question for you is, do you think you were properly prepared to deal with the death of your loved one? I would venture to say that your answer is "no." So do not be too hard on yourself! You were not prepared for this, like most, and the confusion is natural. It is not a sign of your inability or weakness in being confused, fearful, and hurting.

In regard to being prepared for the death of a loved one, I believe the one best resource for help and understanding should be the church. Yet as a professed Christian for over fifty years, I have hardly ever heard the specifics about understanding and preparing for the death of a loved one from the pulpit.

The church has consistently performed their mission to prepare each person spiritually in building a relationship with God and to be in Heaven with Him eternally. But I do not think the church has prepared many people for when they lose a loved one. The church must teach what the Bible says about why God allowed their loved one to be taken from them, to find the answers to the many other questions and challenges that arise from that loss, and to find the comforting promise of peace and hope in one's life now and in the future.

WHAT SHOULD YOU DO ABOUT ADVICE FROM OTHERS?

You will be offered advice as to what you should or should not be doing. Unfortunately, a lot of that well-meaning advice is from people who have not experienced a loss like you have, and do not really understand your reactions are unique to you.

Legitimately, a survivor's response to any suggestions, proposals, opinions, directions, etc. is "In my unique situation, I may not be ready for that solution now, but someday it may apply in my healing."

Because of each person's uniqueness, there is no cookie cutter, one successful way to heal. You must work at it and learn about the grief process and healing and apply what can be useful to heal your unique needs.

SHOULD YOU BE COMPARING YOURSELF TO OTHER SURVIVORS?

There is a tendency for a survivor, and other well-meaning people, to compare the survivor to other survivors in terms of their progression in healing and the time taken for healing. You must be careful not to fall into this trap. No one, including you, should compare how you feel or what you are doing to anyone else because you are unique in your healing.

Your motto should be, **"I will make no comparisons of myself to other survivors because my standard of healing is unique to me."**

Since there is no cookie cutter, one successful way to heal, you must work at it, learn about the process and healing, and apply what is useful to heal your unique needs.

Give yourself a grief break right where you are! You will start to learn how to handle your grief and dig yourself out of this. You are most likely in a very emotional state of mind. Do not think that you are not able to heal and recover a meaningful and fulfilled life! You are okay no matter what your situation is now. You start from here. **YOU CAN DO IT!**

LONELINESS—GRIEF TENDS TO ISOLATE THE SURVIVOR.

Be aware that your grief will tend to isolate you. In fact, it will isolate you more than you think.

Loneliness is one of the most persistent and commonest experiences. It makes sense that you would be lonely as you become more and more isolated.

- **Your loved one and all of the contact with them is gone (emotionally and physically).**
- **Your family and social contacts have and will fall off significantly.**
- **Until you get control of your emotions and your situation (heal somewhat), you do not have the desire nor the energy to get out and be with other people.**

Loneliness will happen! Late in the afternoon, dinner time, the evening; and the weekends become sad and empty.

WHAT DOES LONELINESS SOUND LIKE?

One grief program participant, after losing his wife, said that in the evening, he had never been aware of how loud the antique clocks ticked in his home.

Be careful. Just at the time you need people and their support the most, your grief and confusion tends to push you away from them.

After the visitation, funeral services, internment, and after the cards and flowers, where did everybody go? I just lost my loved one. I am confused, fearful, and hurting, and need caring and support from my loved ones, close friends, my church, and anyone else that will just care. At family gatherings, no one brings up my loved one and the memories! It seems I am no longer invited out to eat or to parties of friends as much or if at all.

It seemed like everyone was so concerned about my welfare and intended to help whenever they could and as soon as they could. But in a short time, no one calls, or no one cares. True, they had all those good intentions, but a survivor must

37

realize that the consensus of the experts is that you lose most of your support within the first year of your survivorship.

I guess it is true when they say that "when a loved one dies, you find out who really loves and/or cares about you,"

It happens, and it is going to happen to you. But in defense of your support people, I think the major reason this valuable and needed support is not forthcoming is they do not know what to say to you or do for you. The easy way out is to do nothing. Remember, neither you, nor them, have been prepared for death and what should or should not be said or done. For instance, have you ever read a book so you would know what to say to someone who has lost a loved one? Here is where you, as the survivor, must fight your disappointment and not let it get the better of you.

Another possible reason you have lost support is that to date, your reactions may have affected the support you have received. You may have been nonresponsive, unpleasant, isolated, sad/depressed, or have not had time because of new responsibilities (i.e., work, children, etc.).

In terms of support, if you have a few people who support you in the right way, you will be blessed. Right away, the average reaction is to think support should come from your closest friends. Not necessarily, your support could come from someone who is a loving, caring person you may meet in a group or elsewhere, particularly in a group of people who are survivors and have experienced what you are going through.

LONELY? HOW TO GET THE MOST QUALITY SUPPORT TO HELP YOU HEAL THE QUICKEST.

I know you do not want to hear this, and in fact, you may not be able to do this right away.

From my experiences and observations, you should get out of the house and be with people, in whatever form, as much and as soon as possible. Other than being with your main support people, your best help is to go to as many gatherings of people who have experienced what you are going through, or any other social gatherings, as soon as possible.

There are several healing advantages to being part of the group experience. First you see and hear what is happening in other survivor's lives. What I have seen in group meetings is that you find out the same crazy thoughts, feelings, and happenings you are experiencing are happening to others. When you hear other survivors talk about what is happening to them, the following results happen:

- **It makes what is going on more natural and less threatening because everyone in the room is experiencing them. Hey, I am not thinking so crazy; or it is not as emotionally threatening as it seems.**
- **Elsewhere in this book, I will discuss how important it is for you to "feel your feelings." You need to inwardly, and most importantly, OUTWARDLY express your feelings. You need to cry, let your anger out (in a positive and appropriate way) as well as your specific pain, frustrations, etc. You can and should express your feelings and needs to your fellow survivors who will understand and, hopefully, encourage and support you and vice versa.**
- **It puts your situation more in perspective because you may find that your situation is not as bad and threatening as it seems. Remember, in a group, there will be survivors who will have less intense losses and some with more intense, hurtful losses. When you hear of some of the messes people are left in, in addition to the pain of losing a loved one, your situation may seem more manageable.**
- **Your relationship with people will be a big part of your healing. (See SMART in chapter 22). Hopefully, one or more of the survivors in any group you par-**

ticipate in will be people you can relate to, build a relationship with, and gain support.
*   Because you are taking the initiative to "move on," it gives you a sense of empowerment, control, and/ or hope.

Get up, get dressed, and get out! Giving love and receiving love heals everything in the long run! You may not feel like you are getting much out of your activities in the beginning; but believe me, you are. You have ramped up your energy to get out, and you have taken some control over recovering your life.

Later in this book, I will give you (exactly) what you need to do to heal and have a meaningful and fulfilled life. But first, you need to understand your grief situation and the emotions you must deal with and what you need to expect will happen. This will reinforce that you are not "going crazy." You are okay. You will get through this!

THE SOONER YOU EMBRACE YOUR NEW LIFE, THE BETTER.

If you think about what has happened, all the circumstances of a survivor's life have changed. Everything they do is different because their loved one is no longer a part of their life and decision-making. Everything, every thought, and every aspect have changed. You are forced into an entirely new life. No wonder there is confusion. No wonder there is fear trying to deal with this totally changed new world.

Because of the magnitude of your loss and the total change in all aspects of your life, I think it is helpful to look at a survivor's situation as having a past life and now a wholly changed **NEW LIFE**. The past life one should take forward with them, honoring it, and never forgetting it. But one's **NEW LIFE** must be looked at and dealt with new eyes and new awareness.

LETTER TO PEOPLE YOU NEED SUPPORT FROM

To My Dear Loved Ones, (family and friends),

I loved _____ so much, and I am devastated by their loss. I do not think I was prepared for their death and all the affects it has on me as the survivor.

I do understand that I will go through many emotions and mood swings over the next period of time. I know that it is healthy and helpful for me to tell you about them and express them outwardly, so please bear with me.

I know it is difficult for you to know what to say to help me. Please know that your presence and prayers are the most important things to me as they speak more to me than words. But remember, experts in the area of grief say that a survivor, even if reticent to do so at first, wants to talk about their loved one and the memories. A survivor may cry and mourn while they reminisce; but all the above is good for their healing. I would welcome this interaction with you.

I know the process of grief will tend to isolate me from fellowship with others, so I need you even more.

I treasure your presence, your caring, your thoughts, and your prayers.

Love, (Signature)

DON'T BE A GRIEF COWBOY OR COWGIRL

If you try to heal by yourself alone, you will suffer more than you need to, and your grief will last longer than it needs to.

The more I experienced grief and subsequently learned about grief, the more I became amazed that people who have lost a loved one and are experiencing the confusion, fear, and pain of grief do not use the sources available to help them heal.

I am saddened by the fact that many survivors are experiencing more hurt and pain than they need to, and they are experiencing such for a longer time, then they need to because they do not seek the proper help.

There is no doubt that when a survivor who is experiencing the process of grief learns how the process of grief works, they will struggle unnecessarily in extensive degrees of greater pain and hurt and experience it for a longer time than they need to.

Let us look at the **survivor who does not read this book or seek help from others who understand the process of grief**. Whatever their situation, without help and understanding, they just keep "Goin' and Doin'" (I will use this term *Goin' and Doin'* from now on to describe the resulting survivor's life without getting any help from anyone or any source and, consequently, never understanding or discovering the answers to the questions (1) How do I heal? and (2) answers to the "why?" that the death of a loved creates and need to be answered to heal and recover life. Finally, time deadens their confusion, fears, and pain to a point where their life is just bearable/livable. (I will use the term *bearable/livable* from now on to describe the quality of a survivor's resulting life if they just keep "Goin' and Doin'" without getting help and healing properly.)

Don't be a grief cowboy or cowgirl ending up with a livable/bearable life but without the meaning, purpose, and hope you could have if you had bothered to learn the answers to the "why" questions your loss created.

CHAPTER 10

HOW THIS BOOK
IS STRUCTURED

A long time ago, I heard a pastor say, "If man knows the WHYS of life, then he can handle the HOWS and HOW COMES of life."

I am writing this book as a survivor who has gone through the healing process of grief. What I am attempting to do is to provide other survivors concrete and specific answers to the many questions that arise about WHY? God allowed this hurtful loss to happen to them, and what can they do to heal?

With a legal and accounting background, it is very import-ant to me to make sense of why things happen. My soul does not rest easy without answers and explanations that are as spe-cific as possible. I approached my loss with the same person-ality. I believe the more a survivor can make sense of why they are experiencing their confusion, fear, and hurt, the easier it is to accept what happened to them and then, additionally, that it had meaning and purpose so their suffering was worthwhile.

I read and researched to make sense of WHY we experience trials and tribulations. WHY DOES GOD LET THIS HAPPEN?

I found that authors have written many books about the loss of a loved one and the grief process. Most of them have a lot of helpful information about how the grief process works (i.e.

what you need to believe, what to expect will happen, and how to heal). But I was still left with major questions.

I felt that Christian writers struggled to provide any clear answers to the major WHY questions survivors have. Their main answer was that a survivor needs to depend on having complete faith in God and should believe

- God is a righteous and good God;
- that He purposes good things to happen for all who are in His purpose;
- that He has the power to make good things happen;
- that He knows everything about you, loves you, and wants good things for you;
- that He is always with you;
- that He has promised He wants good for you, and He will do it.

So the answer was "believe in the goodness of God and have complete faith in His plan for your life ending in good. In the short term, what happened to you now is troubling but have complete faith in this good God, and things will turn out for good in the long run." With that faith, it continues, the survivor will have HOPE for the future, and that hope will provide PEACE and fulfillment in life.

I agreed with all the above statements about God, and a small amount of scripture was quoted to substantiate their truth. So what was my problem?

My faith in God was being sorely tested. I needed to find answers and as much proof as possible to help me make sense out of WHY God let this happen to me and others.

I still had many WHY questions, and I believe many other survivors do too! If they could be answered, the answers would provide a lot more understanding and acceptance, causing increased faith and healing.

The reason that I think it is so important to have the most established and resulting strong faith (created by the most

understanding a survivor can have about God and His character) is because I know that bad times, trials, and tribulations will
come later on in one's life, and in their human weakness, faith
can falter and sometimes even be lost, causing great harm to the
survivor.

Rather than asking a survivor to have faith in God on a
broad basis without much backup scripture to validate the
answers given to have faith and move on to healing and personal
fulfillment, I want to give you answers but also provide you with
scripture proof of the validity of those answers.

Read these scriptures that definitely says that there are
areas that our lesser minds can never understand, and we will
just have to have faith in an all-powerful, well-intentioned, good
God.

> For as the heavens are **higher than the earth**,
> so are **my ways higher than your ways and
> my thoughts than your thoughts**. (Isaiah
> 55:9)

> For **my thoughts are not your thoughts,
> neither are your ways my ways, declares
> the Lord**. (Isaiah 55:8)

> As you do not know the way the Spirit comes
> to the bones in the womb of a woman with
> child, so you do not know the work of God
> who makes everything. (**Ecclesiastics 11:5**)

> But as it is written, **what no eye has seen, nor
> ear heard, nor the heart of man has imag-
> ined, what God has prepared for those who
> love Him.** (**1 Corinthians 2:9–10**)

The above makes sense to me. I see all the wonders God
created every day, and I do not have any trouble believing in

His greatness even though I do not understand it all. I think a survivor can legitimately be asked to have faith in God without total understanding.

But I do not want the above scripture to give any one an easy way out of providing answers to the difficult questions of life.

I will not accept an answer like, "this is such a difficult, confusing situation, and Scripture tells us there are things in our life that we will never understand, so you should accept that and just have faith in God, and let's move on." I only find that answer acceptable when there is an absence of scripture to help give a partial or complete understanding of the situation.

I do not think it is fair to tell a survivor that they just must have total faith in a good God who will always be there for them, and healing will come. Maybe that will work; but I want to reinforce that faith with scriptural proof to ward off troubled times which will come later. I want you to be a survivor who is educated (with a better understanding of God's character and His promises and His actions) and is committed to your decision to follow God, understanding that some faith is required because there are things about God you will never understand.

The more you know, the more you understand; the more sure you are of your decisions, the more committed you are, and the easier it is to stay committed.

A personal confession to you that I learned about myself through my healing process: I have been a professing Christian for over forty-five years (went to church regularly, participated in Bible studies, led a neighborhood Bible study for fifteen plus years, read and studied the Bible periodically); but with all that exposure to God, I still did not really understand what I am going to share with you in this book.

With what I learned in my healing, I started to be able to make sense of why God took my beloved wife and the grief I have experienced. I am now at peace! I want that for you!

I hesitate, but I must ask the question as to whether you and many other professing Christians like me, unless they have experienced some major trial or tragedy and had their relationship and faith in God sorely tested, are knowledgeable enough about what the Bible says about the character of God to muster the faith they need to accept and follow Him through the very bad times of the loss of a loved one.

What I want to do is to confirm in your mind the goodness of God even when He causes or allows bad things to happen. What we must remember is that bad things, unfair trials, and tribulations that are tragedies in our eyes, may make sense in God's eyes because they result in His good purposes.

I intend to give you these proofs with large amounts of scripture. No one should ask you to just have faith, that God is good, and go on with your life trying to heal. I want certain scripture in sections of this book to develop God's character and why He causes or allows things to happen and help you make more sense out of the WHYS of your situation (Scriptural proof of the validity of the answers given).

I found that there are wonderful declarations, illustrations, and examples of who God is and His character that makes happenings and results that do not look fair or loving and/or caring make more sense as to why God let them happen.

As I confessed earlier, I started into the Bible without much understanding of God's character. Then through Scripture, God and the Holy Spirit gave me truth and wisdom to understand God's character and His purpose and my loss. Why is there so much emphasis on Scripture? **God's Word in God's way will help you get your life together more than anything else!** Reading it, studying it, dwelling upon it have opened my mind as to how little I understood God's true character and how He thinks and acts. The Scriptures are more exciting to me now. They sing to me of everything about Him. I feel closer to Him and feel that I now understand Him better and why things happen.

I have not made sense of it all, and the Bible tells me I never will. But the more I know about Him, my Father, the more I think I understand His ways (which helps me understand and accept my losses).

Note: One of the major answers to the WHY question is that God allows things to happen for His glory and for good and to accomplish His eternal purpose (His will). I want you to read a lot of scripture to back up all those statements and help understand God better.

Something you should know is that the three reasons above are not spotlighted and elaborated on by authors like I think they should be. They will be extremely helpful in your understanding, acceptance, and healing.

I want to illustrate what I am saying with an example. Suppose you were going to make an investment into the ownership of a company. The investment is to be substantial, being your life and all your assets. The seller tells you that to gain this ownership, all you have to do is accept the fact that your advisor believes in it; it is a good company with good intentions (purposes) and able to accomplish its purposes, a good investment! All you must do is have total faith in the company and acquire a great investment. Question: how hard would it be to decide to make that investment even with great promises of success just based on faith?

I think it would be unwise and very difficult to "just have faith" and make this lifetime investment. Also, as soon as anything goes wrong, will your faith be strong enough to continue on?

Contrast that investment scenario with another approach. I want you to make that investment, but I want you to research it as much as possible to learn everything you can about that investment first. I believe the more you know about the investment, the better and more committed investment you can make without just relying on outright faith and a much better likelihood of a good result.

To heal, I want you to invest in God's healing power with as much understanding as the Bible can provide. A certain amount of faith will be required because there are areas that we humans will never understand. But there is so much that scripture will help us understand.

DEALING WITH THE EMOTIONS CRISIS

The beginning of healing starts with understanding about and then dealing with the various emotions you are going to experience.

Over a series of conducting grief programs, I learned a valuable lesson. Here I thought I had all this wonderful information and answers to help survivors heal. But I did not realize that until a survivor is able to hear that valuable information, it did not do them any good.

Then it became obvious that as long as a survivor is not aware of their emotional state and trying to understand and deal with it first, they are not in any condition to listen to and hear the other valuable information they need to know, or they are so emotional that they just don't want to listen.

I learned this because participants in my grief programs, who came back for a second time, said they heard and learned so much more because their emotional state was in their way the first time.

That is why it is so important to be aware of and deal with emotions first in one's healing.

The value of dealing with emotions is that the amount of understanding about and proper reactions will help reduce the length and intensity of a survivor's confusion, fear, and hurt.

Here are the things you need to understand about emotions.

1. Even if everything around you was perfect (you had all the questions answered and all the support needed), you will still experience many various emotions in your healing process just because you are human. That's the way you are made.

    Emotions are inherent in our nature and come out naturally when we have a loss. For example, without any training, a baby cries when unhappy.

    So whatever emotions one is experiencing are normal and must necessarily be experienced as a part of human nature.

    The important thing to understand is that one cannot control the things that happen to them, but **one can control how they respond to them**.

2. Because of each survivor's uniqueness, there will be different emotions at different times and in different degrees of intensity. Also, emotional states will last different amounts of time. As you experience and adjust to them, you will be healing bit by bit.

3. You must "**feel your feelings**" and express them as much as possible. You have two choices when you deal with your emotions:

    *   Because one wants to avoid the hurt and pain, one denies or ignores their emotions and hides them away internally. Remember when you bury your emotions, they are buried alive and they will, ultimately, come out later.
    *   Or one recognizes their emotions and how they are feeling and deal with them as quickly as possible.

Denying one's feelings is very unhealthy and a deterrent to healing. Feeling your feelings and dealing with them is the healthiest thing one can do.

Consider the emotion of crying. At the beginning of my "Grieving with Hope" program, everyone is very reticent to cry, particularly men. Yet crying (feeling your feelings) is the healthiest thing one can do. I love to cry. It means I am in tune with my emotions. It releases all the pent-up hurt and pain still present from my loss. After a few sessions in our grief program, most participants cry freely, including the men! It is so healthy to feel your feelings.

I like this piece regarding tears, emotions, and the grief process:

TEARS ARE THE PROOF OF LIFE

"How long will the pain last?" a broken-hearted mourner asked me. "All the rest of your life," I had to answer truthfully. We never quite forget; no matter how many years, we remember.

The loss of a loved one is like a major operation; part of us is removed, and we have a scar for the rest of our lives. This does not mean the pain continues at the same intensity. There is a short while at first when we hardly believe it. It is rather like we have cut our hand; we see the blood flowing, but the pain has not set in yet. When we are bereaved, there is a short while before the pain hits us. But when it does, it is massive in its effect. Grief is shattering.

Gradually, the wound begins to heal. It is like going through a dark tunnel. Occasionally, we glimpse a bit of light up ahead, then we lose sight of it for a while, then we see it again. And then one day, we merge into the light, finally able to laugh, to care, to live. The wound is healed so to speak; the stitches are taken out, and we are whole again but not quite. The scar is still there, and the scar tissue too. As time goes by, we cope. There are things to do, people to care for, tasks that call for our full attention. But the pain is still there, not far below the surface. We see a face that looks familiar, hear a voice that echoes, see a photo in an album, look at a landscape that once we saw together, and it is as though the knife were at the wound again.

But not quite so painfully as at first and now mixed with a little joy too. Remembering a **happy time is not all sorrow; it brings back happiness with it**. How long will the pain last? All the rest of our life. But the thing to remember is that the pain will diminish in intensity even as the memories increase. Tears are the proof of life. The more love, the more tears. And if this be true, then how could we ask that the pain cease altogether? For then the memory of the love would certainly go with it. **The pain of grief is the price of love.**

How effective a survivor is in understanding emotions and dealing with them will determine how intense the confusion, fear, and hurt are and how long the grief healing process will last.

EMOTIONS SEEM TO GO IN THE FOLLOWING SEQUENCE:

SHOCK—"I do not believe it happened!" A sense of unreality or mental confusion surfaces.

DENIAL/DISBELIEF—Refusing to believe it happened, denying it did consciously or subconsciously.

You would not think you would be in denial because everything proves it did happen and is right there in front of you. But it happens. I remember my son was visiting my home shortly after Joyce's death, and he told me he expected her to come walking around the corner any minute. Your ability to recognize self-denial will allow the healing process to begin quicker.

ANGER—It is easy to be angry at God, others and even yourself with all the confusion and hurt being experienced. Self-anger can easily slip into depression. Unchecked anger is probably the major reason for a survivor's rebellion against God and/or society.

Also, one must be very careful that their anger does not express itself on easy targets like friends or family, which helps ruin the support you need.

Anger that is bottled up is like a tea kettle left on a high flame with the top on it. Where there is no outlet for the steam, it will explode.

Remember anger unexpressed can easily become depression.

Remember, you have got to **"feel your feelings"** and express them as much as you can. Little steps at a time!

SADNESS/TEARS—Just existing, overwhelmed by a dark cloud of remorse, unhappiness, and lostness.

The tears will come, whether you want them to or not. It has been nine years, and I still cry often when I start to talk about her loss.

Men and women, let go please. Feel your feelings! Cry as much as you can. It is good for you. Remember the tea kettle!

Crying is the way your eyes speak when your mouth cannot express how much your heart is broken.

F. Alexander Magoun said, "Tears have a wisdom all their own. They come when a person has relaxed enough to let go and to work through his sorrow. They are the natural bleeding of an emotional wound, carrying the poison out of the system. Here lies the road to recovery."

IMMOBILIZATION—A sense of being out of control, powerless, being overwhelmed, numb.

DEPRESSION—Intense sadness to the extent that a survivor becomes unable to function in an ordinary way. Hopelessness seems to paralyze the survivor from wanting to do any of the things they need to do to heal.

LONELINESS—Not a surprising result as the companionship of the loved one is gone, also caused because of the large amount of support being lost.

FEAR—I have to tell you that when I started out my healing journey and until I progressed to researching for my "Grieving with Hope" program that I did not realize how prominent the emotion of fear is in a survivor. Fear is the quiet stranger in the equation. It is always there and very disconcerting. There is fear of what is going to happen today (something new seems to crop up daily), the major fear of the unknown in the future (particularly because of all that has been lost and the significant changes that have happened), and the fear of failure.

PAIN/HURT—We have this emotion even when the cause of it was something minor. Our loved one's death was major, so it is only natural to feel an exaggerated hurt and lasting longer than we would naturally anticipate. No matter how long your hurt lasts, you are okay emotionally. That is just your unique way of healing.

UNFAIRNESS—How could this happen to me? Unfairness impacts the whole basis of one's belief system. In fact, isn't fairness an attribute of our life we have wanted from the beginning, a desire for God and the world to just be fair? When something as unfair as this happens to us, it rips away all our security and nibbles at our future hopes and dreams.

CONFUSION—We have already reviewed how such a great loss and change in your life explains any confusion that arises. Understand it, and accept that you are "okay" even though you seem confused. Then you can begin to take action to eliminate it!

TOWARD GOD
Testing God
Bargaining with God

GUILTY FEELINGS

Regrets—Because you did or did not do something.

Relief—That health care does not have to be provided anymore, that the troublesome situation is over.

Resentment—That your loved one left you and/or the mess you were left in.

ANXIETY
PANIC
BROKENNESS
HOPELESSNESS
DOUBT
FRUSTRATION
DISAPPOINTMENT

OTHER PHYSICAL AND MEDICAL EFFECTS OF EMOTIONS

- Appetite change
- Nausea
- Weight gain/loss
- Loss of taste/smell
- Insomnia/interrupted sleep
- Extreme fatigue/exhaustion
- Shortness of breath

- Chest pain
- Muscular tension/backaches
- Headaches

Identify your emotions and accept that exaggerated emotions are not a sign of incompetence or weakness. You are human, and these emotions are **natural**. Yes, they are very **necessary** for you to experience. You must ultimately deal with your emotional state, learn about yourself and heal, hopefully, to a meaningful and fulfilled new life.

I thought this "Tangled Ball of Emotions" by H. Norman Wright pretty much illustrates exactly how a survivor's mental state is at the beginning.

GRIEF

A TANGLED BALL OF EMOTIONS

BY: H. NORMAN WRIGHT

In addition, the enclosed chart has been adapted from Elizabeth Kubler-Ross's work on the cycle of grief. It illustrates phases of the grief process from the top left, the **Beginning/ Denial Stage**, down to the **Resistance Stage**. From there, it illustrates the beginning of healing and its attitude and activities in the **Exploration Stage** (in the lower right corner). Then it proceeds up to the **Commitment to Healing Stage to a New Life**.

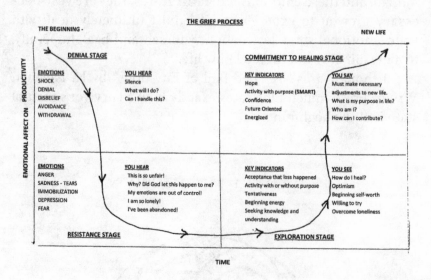

Where are you on this chart now? Make sure you look at it closely. **Keep this chart**. There are some good criteria to judge how you are healing! Pay attention to what you are hearing, seeing, and saying!

Take advantage of these **Twelve Freedoms of Healing**:

- You have the FREEDOM to realize your grief is unique.
- You have the FREEDOM to talk about your grief.
- You have the FREEDOM to feel a multitude of emotions.
- You have the FREEDOM to allow for numbness.
- You have the FREEDOM to feel grief attacks or memory embraces.
- You have the FREEDOM to develop a support system.
- You have the FREEDOM to make use of ritual.

- You have the FREEDOM to embrace your spirituality.
- You have the FREEDOM to search for meaning.
- You have the FREEDOM to treasure your memories.
- You have the FREEDOM to move toward your grief and heal. (*Understanding Grief* by Alan D. Wolfelt, PhD)

As you experience these freedoms and a softening of your emotions, you will start to hear things that make sense to you. Soon, you will get out of the pit of **"no energy, no care."** And you will start going to activities and doing things you need to do to recover life.

THE DILEMMA OF SHOULD A SURVIVOR TALK ABOUT THEIR FEELINGS, AND IF SO, HOW MUCH?

Should you talk about your situation?

You are finding that even though people ask, "How are you doing?" you do not tell them how you really feel. You do not want to burden them with your problems.

Also, you are finding even though people ask, "Do you need something?" when you reach the point where you actually know what help you need, you do not tell them your needs because you do not want to burden them with your problems. Do you see a trend here?

There are three important aspects of why the survivor needs to speak out and act out about how they are feeling emotionally and physically. The first is, a survivor needs to understand they have a great need to be **heard** and **authenticated**.

Advisors with experience agree. They say the best thing that could happen to a survivor, who is feeling their feelings, is they put their thoughts and feelings into **words** and **constructive actions** and **express them**.

If a survivor is unable to verbalize and express their feelings, they are left feeling that they are misunderstood, isolated, and insecure.

Being authenticated means the survivor is listened to and supported at their level of words and actions. That level may not be totally correct, but it is **accepting "where a survivor is,"** and that's the best place to start healing.

That is why support people are so important. They must just "be there" with the survivor, listening, listening, listening, and accepting the survivor where they are.

The second major factor is that it's a well-accepted observation that a **survivor really wants to talk about their loss and their feelings**. In fact, they need to express what's happening to them to alleviate the frustrations and buildup of emotions with no outlet.

Survivors want to talk about their loved one and the memories, maybe hesitantly at first but heartily later. If you were a counselor, doesn't that seem to be the best therapy? Accept your loss and talk about it; and express your feelings and concerns so you can start your healing.

Question: If a survivor understands that turning their emotions into words and voicing them is a major factor in their healing, why is it so hard to do? If survivors really want to talk about their situation, why don't they do it more?

Expressing one's feelings is difficult because

- you are afraid your emotional state will show weakness or the inability to handle your situation. You are afraid you are not being **strong**;
- you do not want to be embarrassed, or feel uncomfortable, by becoming emotional, breaking down (crying), and sharing your real feelings, anger, or depression;

- you do not want to impose on anyone by upsetting them emotionally in talking about the loss or creating an obligation for the listener to help because they were told of the need;
- Of fear of the unknown.

Perhaps you identify with some of these reasons. They are legitimate reasons. You just must overcome them so you can express yourself in a way you need to, to heal.

The elephant will be in the room for a long time. Do what is best for you and the people there and poke the elephant and say something like, "I really miss my loved one. I am healing and dealing with my new life; but I never want to forget my loved one, so please feel free to talk about them with me. I treasure the memories."

In fact, my biggest mistake going through my loss is I never opened up conversations about my wife with our children and close family.

It is not too hard to figure out why. I was into myself and had to learn how to heal. I did not know until later that I should have helped my family by expressing my feelings and helping them to start their healing too. Hey! Do not wait! You and your family will heal quicker if you talk about everything.

Not talking about your loss with your support people is detrimental to your healing. Be aware. The survivor loses a lot of needed support from family and friends because they are afraid to talk about their loss because it may make someone uncomfortable.

I have said your loss of support could be because either you or your support do not know what to say, so everything is left all unsaid and undone. Remember, your closest and most important support groups may be going through their own process of grief, they could be emotionally crippled and are not able to reach out to help you even though they want to—a very valid reason why they have not met your expectations. In every situation, you must ask, how have they been affected, and where are they in the grief healing process?

The third thing a survivor needs to understand is the subtlety of **the repression of the expressions of grief.** Don't feel bad because you find it so hard to find outlets to express how you are really feeling. It takes a lot of searching to find listening ears to help you heal. Why is it so hard to get help?

What you must recognize is that we live in a society whose goals are happiness and success. A subject like grief entails negative characteristics like the confusion, fear, and hurt of losing a loved one and is **very uncomfortable** for society to deal with. Consequently, the world has little patience with malingering sadness and negative results. The world is not very patient and wants you to get this unhappy, confusing process of grief to be over with as soon as possible.

Unfortunately, the Christian church has also leaned toward the doctrines of peace, happiness, and positive living. It too has become impatient with lingering sadness and negative happenings.

Christian beliefs have the power to uphold a survivor and provide the meaning and purpose which will heal them. But when was the last time you heard Christian leaders highlight God's provisions that help heal for those who have lost a loved one? Besides, reinforcing the need for a part of the body of Christ to support a survivor with the time, energy, and patience is needed to be given sacrificially to help them heal.

The result? Society and even the loving and caring Christian community are not prioritizing the care, time, and attention needed for a group of very needy survivors.

Result: The above highlights what you should expect as far as support from any large amount of people and how important an individual support person is to healing.

CHAPTER **13**

FACED WITH THE CAPABILITY CRISIS

CONFRONTING THE SECOND STAGE IN HEALING
AM I CAPABLE OF HANDLING THIS CONFUSING MESS I HAVE
BEEN HANDED?

As if dealing with the **EMOTIONAL CRISIS** of loss was not enough, consider the "residue" that takes front stage.

Survivors are left with all the personal, family, and business affairs to handle, usually on their own. Sometimes this challenging situation can be handled. However, many times their responsibilities leave the survivor thinking they are incapable of handling all they must do, which just adds to the confusion, fear, and hurt condition they are already in.

Why wouldn't a survivor have a **CAPABILITY CRISIS**? A lot of their responsibilities are brand new to them. They have little or no knowledge about them. Consequently, one makes mistakes. In addition, many areas must be acted on almost immediately because of their nature. Immediacy compounds the lack of knowledge and experience and fear of failure.

Unless one handled these affairs before, being handed all of this has got to be overwhelming without knowledgeable help.

Frankly, without experience, a survivor is not capable of doing a very good job.

The ideal effect of this book would be for the survivor to learn about, understand, and be able to deal with their emotions (heal) as quickly as they can. Any degree of healing of emotions will then help a survivor deal with the everyday problems and decisions they are faced with in their **CAPABILITY CRISIS**.

Unfortunately, some decisions and actions must be taken before a survivor can completely and effectively deal with their emotions. I think the best advice is to only make decisions if you absolutely must, but be sure and ask for help from a knowledgeable friend or expert adviser in doing so. The more one is emotionally stable, the better everyday decisions are made.

I would recommend that any major decisions and/or changes a survivor makes should be deferred at least one year.

I have observed that as this crisis develops, the survivor becomes even more agitated, causing them more confusion and doubting of their capabilities. Then they begin to show signs of anger and irritability because no one seems to be helping them.

Survivors also have other capability concerns arise. One that I heard almost every meeting was **"I have got to be strong"** for my family and the people around me. Yet realistically, most survivors must wonder if they will ever be able to be strong when their life seems to be in great confusion. Also, they wonder if they are capable of holding together all the interpersonal relationships that are important and needed because most everything is not going very well.

All are valid reasons why a survivor starts doubting themselves, and they do.

I will provide information on how to deal with this **CAPABILITY CRISIS** and the next **CHARACTER CRISIS** in chapter 16.

CHAPTER 14

THE THIRD STEP IN THE GRIEF HEALING PROCESS, THE CHARACTER CRISIS—WHO AM I?

Along with dealing with your **EMOTIONAL CRISIS** with its ups and downs and resulting confusion, one has to wander through confronting their **CAPABILITY CRISIS**. (Can I handle this mess they handed me without falling apart?) This will subtly lead into a **CHARACTER CRISIS**, undermining a survivor's confidence in themselves.

"Who am I now?" Your identity has been shattered. You have experienced a tremendous loss, major change, and a future life alone. In that condition, one starts struggling with their identity, their worth, and the strength of their total character.

Character and confidence questions come up:

- Do I personally have anything of value to contribute to anyone or anything now or in the future?
- Do I have any worth?

- Did my identity and value depend on me or my loved one's influence? If my loved one was a significant part of my identity, what do I do to establish my own identity?
- Is my character strong enough to persist and heal? Or am I going to fall apart?
- I have observed this crisis happening in many different ways, but when confidence wanes and self-doubt sets in:
- it becomes harder to make decisions, so decisions are deferred, slowed down, or not made at all;
- it becomes harder to do activities, particularly ones crucial to the healing process;
- the survivor slows down and draws back from their responsibilities and things they should be doing;
- in avoiding things, the survivor isolates themselves even more;
- a reticence to be around other people is felt because of a lack of confidence;
- the survivor starts to feel insignificant, uninteresting, and unworthy. They wonder if they have anything of worth to offer life and others;
- the survivor starts to feel resentful because they are lonely with little or no help.

Losing one's confidence is tough enough in regular life, but it is devastating in the midst of the grief healing process. Right when a survivor needs to be that "strong" that they want to be and really believing in themselves and their judgment, they are faltering.

How can you overcome the **CAPABILITY CRISIS** and the **CHARACTER CRISIS**? We will explore a concept that is invaluable in every aspect of daily living. You should take it to heart and apply it every day, particularly when one is experiencing trials and tribulations that are causing them to question their capabilities and/or character.

In the next chapter, I will provide the answer on how to overcome the CAPABILITY CRISIS and the **CHARACTER CRISIS** with a concept that is invaluable in every aspect of daily living (you should take it to heart and apply it every day) and, particularly, when one is experiencing trials and tribulations that are causing them to question their capabilities and/or character.

CHAPTER **15**

WHAT YOU NEED TO KNOW TO OVERCOME THE CAPABILITY AND CHARACTER CRISIS

If you are confronted with these two crises, I would venture to say that you are probably not feeling very confident in your abilities right now.

There is not much happening to support you and build you up. You wonder if you are loved, if you are able to handle things, who you really are, if you are worthy, what you have to offer life and the people around you, and on and on.

Confusion, fear, and hurt of grief is causing you to start to lose your confidence and questioning your worthiness. Then the world compounds these negative thoughts, particularly through commercials, by telling you what you personally lack and how needy you are. Your whole environment is definitely not supporting you and adding to that **"gotta be strong" attitude you want and need**.

Where does my help come from? It comes from the Lord!

What you need to know and have reinforced is that **THERE IS SOMETHING VERY SPECIAL ABOUT YOU. YOU NEED TO BE REMINDED HOW SPECIAL AND IMPORTANT YOU ARE AND WHY!**

Now is the time for you to understand why you are special and how it helps your healing.

What you will be reminded of here will **HELP YOU OVERCOME ANY AND ALL OF THE CONFUSION, DOUBT, AND FEARS YOU HAVE, EMBRACE WHO YOU REALLY ARE INTO YOUR MIND AND SOUL, HAVE CONFIDENCE THAT YOU ARE AS SPECIAL AS SHOWN HERE, WHICH WILL GIVE YOU THE CONFIDENCE AND STRENGTH TO MOVE ON.**

YOU ARE SPECIAL BECAUSE OF THE FOLLOWING REASONS:

1. GOD KNOWS YOUR NAME AND LOVES YOU MORE THAN YOU CAN IMAGINE.

   Neither death nor life, nor angels nor rulers, nor things present, nor things to come... **Nor anything else in all creation will be able to separate us from the love of God that is in Christ Jesus, our Lord**. (Romans 8:35–37)

   When the righteous cry for help, the Lord hears and delivers them out of all their troubles. (**Psalm 34:18**)

   God puts your tears in a bottle. (**Psalm 56:8**)

   God numbers every hair on your head. (**Luke 12:7, Matthew 10:30**)

   Precious in the sight of the Lord is the death of his saints. (Psalm 116:15)

For he who touches you touches the apple of His eye. (**Zechariah 2:8**)

I have loved you with an everlasting love; therefore, I have continued my faithfulness to you. (Jeremiah 31:3)

2.   THE AMAZING THING ABOUT YOU IS THIS ALMIGHTY AND POWERFUL GOD CHOSE YOU TO BE HIS CHILD.

Blessed be the God and Father of our Lord Jesus Christ who has blessed us in Christ with every spiritual blessing in the heavenly places even as **he chose us in Him before the foundation of the world** that we should be holy and blameless before Him. In love, **He predestined us for adoption** as sons through Jesus Christ **according to the purpose of His will** to the praise of His glorious grace with which He has blessed us in the beloved. In Him, we have redemption through His blood, the forgiveness of our trespasses according to the riches of **His grace, which He lavished upon us in all wisdom and insight, making known to us the mystery of His will according to His purpose**, which He set forth in Christ as a plan for the fullness of time to unite all things in Him, things in Heaven and things on earth. (**Ephesians 1:3–10**)

For you formed my inward parts, you knitted me together in my mother's womb. I praise you, for I am fearfully and wonderfully made. Wonderful are your works; my soul knows it very well. **My frame was not hidden from you when I was being made in**

71

secret, intricately woven in the depths of the earth. Your eyes saw my unformed substance; in your Book were written, every one of them, the days that were formed for me when as yet there were none of them. (Psalm 139:13–16)

For those whom He foreknew, He also predestined to be conformed to the image of His Son in order that He might be the firstborn among many brothers. And those whom He predestined He also called, and those whom He called He also justified, and those He justified He also glorified. (**Romans 8:29–30**)

And My servant whom I have chosen... because you are precious in My eyes, and honored, and I love you. (**Isaiah 43:4**)

Fear not, I am the one who helps you. (**Isaiah 41:13**)

I knew you even before you were conceived. Before I formed you in the womb, I knew you, and before you were born, I consecrated you... (**Jeremiah 1:5**)

3. GOD PROMISES TO PROTECT YOU AND TO GIVE YOU STRENGTH IN TIMES OF NEED.

Fear not; for I am with you; be not dismayed, for I am your God; I will strengthen you. I will help you; I will uphold you with my righteousness right hand. (**Isaiah 41:10**)

**The Lord is near to the brokenhearted and saves those who are crushed in spirit.
(Psalm 34:18)**

Blessed are those who mourn, for they shall be comforted. (Matthew 5:4)

Do not be frightened, and do not be dismayed, for the Lord your God is with you wherever you go. **(Joshua 1:9)**

In returning (to God) and rest, you shall be saved; in quietness and in trust (in God) shall be your strength. **(Isaiah 30:15)**

My grace is sufficient for you, for **my power is made perfect in weakness**. Therefore, I will boast all the more gladly of my weaknesses so that the power of Christ may rest upon me. For the sake of Christ, then I am **content with weaknesses, insults, hardships, persecutions, and calamities. For when I am weak, then I am strong. (2 Corinthians 12:8–10)**

Cast your burden on the Lord, and He will sustain you. (Psalm 55:22)

The Lord is my strength and my shield, my heart trusts in Him. **(Psalm 28:7)**

Though I walk in the midst of trouble, you preserve my life. (Psalm 138:7)

I will say to the Lord, "My refuge and my fortress, my God, in whom I trust." **(Psalm 91:2)**

Blessed be the God and Father of our Lord Jesus Christ, the Father of all mercies and God **of all comfort** who comforts us in **all our afflictions**... (**2 Corinthians 1:3–4**)

He will cover you with His pinions, and under His wings, you will find refuge; His faithfulness is a shield and buckler. (**Psalm 91:4**)

For He will command His angels concerning you to guard you in all your ways. (**Psalm 91:11**)

(God says about the believer)—"Because he holds fast to Me in love, I will deliver him; **I will protect him** because he knows my name. When he calls to me, I will answer him; **I will be with him in trouble**; I will rescue him and honor him. With long life, I will satisfy him and show him my salvation. (**Psalm 91:14–16**)

Then shall your (God's) light break forth like the dawn, and Your (God's) healing shall spring up speedily. (**Isaiah 58:8**)

God is our refuge and strength, a very present help in trouble. Therefore, we will not fear though the earth gives way, though the mountains be moved into the heart of the sea. (**Psalm 46:1–2**)

...I am the Lord, your healer. (**Exodus 15:26**)

He sent out His Word and healed them. (**Psalm 107:20**)

I will not leave you as orphans; I will come to you. (John 14:18)

...the grace of God that was given you in Christ Jesus that in every way you were enriched in Him in all speech and all knowledge so that you are not lacking in any gift as you wait for the revealing of our Lord Jesus Christ who will sustain you to the end. (**1 Corinthians 1:7**)

He gives power to the faint, and to him who has no might, He increases strength. (**Isaiah 40:29**)

But they who wait for the Lord shall renew their strength; they shall mount up with wings like eagles; **they shall run and not be weary; they shall walk and not faint.** (Isaiah 40:31)

As for me, I am poor and needy, but the Lord takes thought for me. (**Psalm 40:17**)

You keep him in perfect peace whose mind is stayed on you. (Isaiah 26:3–4)

...I came that they might have life and have it abundantly. (John 10:10)

When you pass through the waters, I will be with you; and through the rivers, they shall not overwhelm you; when you walk through fire, you shall not be burned, and the flame shall not consume you. (**Isaiah 43:2–3**)

Peace I leave with you; My peace I give to you. Let not your hearts be troubled, neither let them be afraid. (John 14:27)

He restores my soul. (**Psalm 23:3**)

My presence shall go with thee, and I shall give you rest. (**Exodus 33:14**)

The Lord upholds all who are falling and raises up all who are bowed down. (Psalm 145:14)

The Lord is near to all who call on Him, to all who call on Him in truth. (**Psalm 145:18**)

He fulfills the desire of those who fear Him; **He also hears their cry and saves them. (Psalm 145:19)**

One thing have I asked of the Lord, that will I seek after that I may dwell in the house of the Lord all the days of my life,....**for he will hide me in His shelter in the day of trouble;** He will conceal me under the cover of His tent; He will lift me high upon a rock. (**Psalm 27:4–6**)

Come to me, all who labor and are heavy laden, and I will give you rest. Take my yoke upon you, and learn from me, for I am gentle and lowly in heart, and you will find rest for your souls. For my yoke is easy, and my burden is light. (**Matthew 11:28–30**)

4. YOU MAY WONDER WHERE GOD'S PROMISES OF LOV-
   ING YOU AND PROTECTING YOU ARE AND WHY YOU
   ARE SUFFERING. WHERE IS HIS HELP? DOES HE STILL
   CARE? REMEMBER THIS, HE PROMISES NEVER TO
   LEAVE OR FORSAKE YOU!

For **He has said, I will never leave you nor
forsake you.** (Hebrews 13:5)

Blessed is the man whom You discipline, O
Lord, and whom you teach out of your law to
give him rest from days of trouble until a pit
is dug for the wicked. For **the Lord will not
forsake His people**, He will not abandon His
heritage. (**Psalm 94:12–14**)

**Who shall separate us from the love of
Christ? Shall tribulation, or persecution,
or famine, or nakedness, or danger, or
sword**: no, in all these things we are more
than conquerors through Him who loved us.
For I am sure that neither death nor life,
nor angels, nor rulers, nor things present, nor
things to come, nor powers, nor height, nor
depth... **Nor anything else in all creation
will be able to separate us from the love
of God that is in Christ Jesus, our Lord.**
(**Romans 8:35–37**)

So when God desired to show more con-
vincingly to the heirs of the promise the
unchangeable character of his purpose,
He guaranteed it with an oath so that by two
unchangeable things in which it is impossible
for God to lie, we who have fled for refuge
might have strong encouragement **to hold**

fast to the hope set before us. We have this (promise) as a sure and steadfast anchor of the soul. (Hebrews 6:17–19)

Give thanks to the Lord of hosts for the Lord is good, for His steadfast love endures forever. **(Jeremiah 33:11)**

I will be with you, I will not leave you or forsake you. **(Joshua 1:5)**

...And behold, I am with you always to the end of the age. **(Matthew 28:20)**

Trust in the Lord forever, for the Lord God is an everlasting rock. **(Isaiah 26:4)**

I will not forget you. **(Isaiah 49:15)**

I hope the above confirms in your mind HOW LOVED AND HOW SPECIAL AND CAPABLE YOU ARE. No matter how you feel and your current situation challenges you, no matter what doubts you have, you have a Father God WHO LOVES YOU AND EQUIPPED YOU TO HANDLE ANY SITUATION.

Also, recognize that because you are so special that YOU ARE STILL HERE FOR A REASON AND PURPOSE THAT GOD HAS FOR YOU! HE HAS PROVIDED YOU WITH ALL YOU NEED TO ACCOMPLISH HIS PURPOSE.

Take His love and promises, and let them touch your heart and reinforce that you are LOVED, WORTHY, AND ABLE TO GET THROUGH THESE VERY DIFFICULT TIMES, NO MATTER WHAT.

No matter how lonely, no matter how low you feel emotionally, no matter how incapable you feel, God is always there for you and to support you.

I HOPE YOU SEE HOW IMPORTANT KNOWING THAT GOD'S LOVE FOR YOU AND HIS PROMISES TO YOU ARE ALWAYS THERE IS FOR EACH INDIVIDUAL, knowing the above should give each person **hope and the confidence to take on any of the future challenges of life facing them.**

To tell the truth, I do not think that most Christians have understood and are applying this powerful truth in their daily lives. But when trials and tribulations come, they are finally challenged, they become concerned, experience self-doubts, and are exposed to how important their understanding of who they are (their self-image) and where their support and enabling comes from (a loving and protecting God) for their recovery and healing.

Please recall that ONE OF THE MAIN GOALS of this book is that you would walk away from it FEELING SPECIAL, LOVED, ENABLED, WORTHY, PROTECTED, AND STRENGTHENED, that wonderful self-assurance coming from God and His Word will always be there, in the best and the worst of times, to validate and encourage each person TO BE PERSISTENT IN LIFE. PERSISTENCE BECOMES CHARACTER, AND CHARACTER BECOMES HOPE.

EVERY ONE OF US NEEDS TO REVIEW AND REINFORCE HOW SPECIAL AND LOVED WE ARE BY GOD WITH HIS SCRIPTURE FREQUENTLY.

CHAPTER 16

DEALING WITH THE SPIRITUAL CRISIS

ARE YOU GOING TO TRY TO RECOVER WITH OR WITHOUT GOD?

First of all, I believe that you will only heal and have a new life that is meaningful and fulfilled if you can find acceptable answers to your **"WHY"** questions about the following:

- **Why** would a loving God let this happen?
- **Why** did this happen to me?
- Did I do something wrong?
- Did my loved one do something wrong?
- **Why** is God silent when I need Him most?

Then there are the questions about the future:

- What should I do now? What is my purpose?
- How can I function with a big part of my life gone?
- Who am I really?
- What is going to happen to me?

The more acceptable the answers to the "**WHY**" questions, the more it will help you make better sense of what happened. Making as much sense as you can will put meaning and purpose into your life. With meaning and purpose, you will have hope, and hope will mature into your healing and the peace in your life that I am sure you want more than anything.

HEALING WITHOUT GOD, YOUR EYES ARE ON YOURSELF ALONE, AND YOUR SUCCESS IS TOTALLY DEPENDENT ON YOU.

How does the choice without God look? First of all, without God, there is not even any attempt to give any meaning or purpose to why your loved one died. That is one of your biggest "**WHY**" questions, but there is no apparent explanation to be found without God. **It just happened.** Your loss was just a random happening in the travails/turmoil of life. If you want to try to put any meaning to your loved one's life and loss, you have to hope that they left some good result in their legacy or that they inspired some good activities by their family (spouse, children, grandchildren, etc.) or friends.

Without God, your loss just seems to be bad luck, very unfair, and no discernible reason or purpose in why your loved one died, except it resulted in your confusion, fear, and hurt.

Plus, there is no future promise, and resulting hope, that you will one day be with God and with your loved ones in Heaven for eternity.

- I believe the following puts life and death in proper perspective:
- Without a creator, there is no design or purpose in what happens. So what happens is random and, ultimately, meaningless.
- God is the only absolute in a world of relativity.
- Without God, we are a mistake floating in a mistake.

- Without God, we are trapped in the blind forces (which may not love you), which are merciless and cold, subjecting us to an impersonable fate.

Choosing a path of healing and a new life that has no meaning and purpose in it is like getting in your car in Ohio and hoping to get to Disney World in Florida with no map, GPS, or other form of direction. You will have to drive south (Goin' and Doin') and just see what happens—no direction, not knowing what to anticipate. **If you do not stop and get help, you will probably never find what you seek!**

My conclusion when my faith was tested was that without God, I could not find any meaning and purpose that would give me the understanding and hope that would make my new life meaningful and fulfilled.

CHOOSING TO HEAL WITH GOD—YOUR EYES ARE ON GOD—THERE IS DESIGN, PURPOSE, LOVE, PROMISES, HOPE.

Maybe you have found the answers to life and death already; but if not, you have found what you have been searching for in this book—design, purpose, love, hope, and peace.

When you understand and accept the fact that you are **loved more than you can imagine, and you are a special individual who is part of God's design and purpose** (His Eternal Plan for His children), then you will find meaning and purpose, which will give you hope, peace, and fulfillment in your new life.

Your hope and faith in God will be reinforced because the Bible tells us His purpose in everything that happens is for **good**. (Don't we all want good results if we can have it?) And the ultimate good is that God is given the glory, and His Gospel of salvation is being spread by His children, and His incomparable love is being shared.

And what does God promise? Death is **no longer an end** because we will have **eternal life with God someday**.

We will be with our Father/God and loved ones in Heaven for eternity.

WHY SHOULD WE DEPEND ON THIS GOD OF THE BIBLE AND HIS WORD?

WHO IS THIS GOD?

CREATOR—In His infinite wisdom, God created everything, including us, which means we belong to Him.

RULER—God sustains the universe, keeping it intact. He is sovereign over everything, therefore, has control of all things. Nothing happens unless God allows it.

FATHER—God loves us enough to pursue us when we were in rebellion against Him and paid the penalty so we could come back to Him like the prodigal son. He loves us, and He is gracious.

COUNSELOR—God is all-knowing and promises to guide and comfort us.

A BIBLICAL PERSPECTIVE OF GOD

Scripture is the only place to learn about God and His character. The Bible gives us an insight into God's character. It does not say these are true only when things are going well. If you believe them when things are good, you must believe them when things seem bad:

LOVING	MEASURELESS	CHANGELESS
TIMELESS	WISE	FORGIVING
PRESENT	MAJESTIC	FAITHFUL
SPOTLESS	AVAILABLE	POWERFUL
GLORIOUS	MIGHTY	SECURE
GREAT	STEADFAST	PEACEFUL
HOLY	WONDERFUL	RIGHTEOUS
PATIENT	JUST	MERCIFUL
GRACIOUS	INVINCIBLE	JOY
RELIABLE	GENEROUS	INFINITE
STRONG	KIND	STABLE
SUFFICIENT	RESPONSIVE	ACCESSIBLE

...Blessed are You, O Lord, the God of Israel, our father, forever and ever. Yours, O Lord, is the **greatness and the power and the glory and the victory and the majesty**, for all that is in the heavens and in the earth is yours. Yours is the kingdom, O Lord, and You are exalted as head above all. Both riches and honor come from You, and You rule over all. In Your hand are power and might, and in Your hand, it is to make great and to give strength to all. And now we thank You, our God, and praise Your glorious name. (**1 Chronicles 29:10-13**)

85

Is this the kind of father you could really love and commit your healing and life to?

> ...Father of mercies and God of all comfort...
> (**2 Corinthians 1:3**)

> Then you shall call, and the Lord will answer; you shall cry, and He will say "Here I am."
> (**Isaiah 58:9**)

> God is our refuge and strength, a very present help in trouble. Therefore, we will not fear though the earth gives way, though the mountains be moved into the heart of the sea.
> (**Psalm 46:1–2**)

CHAPTER 18

NEGOTIATING THE REALISTIC EXPECTATIONS CRISIS

From the beginning, a survivor has to deal with the **EMOTIONAL CRISIS** and the **CAPABILITY CRISIS** soon to find out that a **CHARACTER CRISIS** follows closely behind. On top of that, they have to learn how to form **REALISTIC EXPECTATIONS** as to what is going to happen to them in their healing process.

A survivor who was not prepared for their loss and does not know how the grief process works tends to have expectations as to what will happen to them in the healing process—expectations that are too idealistic and lacking the reality of what is really going to happen to them.

Unrealistically, high expectation results in many disappointments and failures that do not have to be experienced. Forming realistic expectations is especially important to reduce confusion, fear, and hurt and speed healing.

In addition to forming unrealistically high expectations, a survivor is faced with unexpected disruptive surprises that happen to them that they were not aware would happen and are totally unprepared for.

Now add the aspect that most, if not all, survivors are not prepared for the death of a loved one and have no experience with losing a loved one or any idea what to expect will happen in the future, you have a situation destined for big disappointments.

Thus, a survivor needs to know that the sooner they learn about the grief process and listen to survivors who have experienced grief, they will be more able to form more realistic expectations.

Listed below are some areas where a survivor needs to form as realistic expectations as possible about.

- One of the best examples of a common unrealistic expectation that survivors form is that **there will be a lot of support**. Why not expect support? All the people at the viewing and burial service offering help—all the family members and friends, the neighbors, the church, and on and on. Most are good people and care about you and meant their offers of support. **But where did everybody go?**

  What really happens? Experience shows that 75 percent of your possible support is gone within thirty days. In fact, a survivor is fortunate if they end up with at least one person who is really lending support, time, and energy to the survivor.

  High, unrealistic expectations of support are dashed by the reality of the tremendous loss of support, resulting in the survivor feeling neglected and substantially hurt by the result. With proper realistic expectations, a survivor can avoid a lot of disappointment and hurt!

- Dealing with your grief and your various crises is going to cause you to experience **ABNORMAL PHYSICAL AND MENTAL ACTIONS.** You will not be the same as before. You will be thinking and doing new weird things—for example, wondering if you are going crazy, forgetting things, lacking interest in life, etc. Understand, anticipate, and accept that your **INITIAL ABNORMAL**

BEHAVIOR IS NORMAL as you start to deal with grief. No matter what happens, **you are okay for now (and will be)**.

One survivor told me that in their troubled state, they did not hear much at first in the grief meetings. But the most important thing they heard was that their different and disturbing actions were **NORMAL**, and **"they were okay for now right where they were."**

- Grief tends to isolate you. With the amount of loss of support and the tendency to not want to get out with other people, a survivor frequently ends up alone and lonely (especially at dinnertime, in the evening, and on weekends).

- Experiencing grief will take more energy than you expect. Recognize that you will be tired and will lack energy for a while.

- Your grief will last longer than you think. Other people will have a time line for recovery for you; but you have your own unique time line, and it will not happen until then.

- People do not know what to say to you or how to help you. So they do not do anything. That ends up in confusion and hurt for you. To help illustrate why this happened and how normal it is, I ask you: Since like other people you were not prepared for losing a loved one, do you know what to say or do for someone else who has lost a loved one? I venture to say the answer is no, thus, great silence and confusion, on both sides of a death.

  At some time, you need to make it a point to learn what to say and do to help other survivors because you are now uniquely qualified to help them more than anyone else.

- All spheres of your life will be affected: intellectual, physical, emotional, and spiritual.

89

- A survivor usually does not realize what they have lost. The first thing experienced is the loss of companionship of their loved one, then the realization that they have lost all of the hopes and dreams for the future they had together, then the reality of current needs and problems unmet will cause more confusion, fear, and hurt (CAPABILITY CRISIS). You must be aware and prepared because life will pop up and slap you in the face with these reminders!

- Aspects of your healing process will change frequently. There will be ups and downs emotionally in many different and exaggerated ways, particularly on holidays, anniversaries, and special days. It will not be smooth. Unexpected changes in your emotions do not make your actions wrong. You are still okay!

- You may experience trouble with concentration, memory, and decision-making. It will be okay!

- You may find yourself acting socially in ways that are different from before. Your uniqueness makes that okay in the beginning process of your healing!

- You may begin a search for meaning and purpose and may question your religion and philosophy of life.

  My hope is that a survivor will be aware and form expectations about the above-mentioned areas that are as realistic as possible.

THE "WHY" QUESTIONS CRISIS

Okay, you have read about the **EMOTIONAL CRISIS** you will face. You must understand, be aware of, and deal with your emotions as soon as possible. However, I have learned that dealing with your emotions, and even to the point of emotional healing, is only one-half of a survivor's journey. What I have observed is that without the second half of the grief journey (getting the answers to their WHY) questions, a survivor just continues on "Goin' and Doin'" as best they can and end up with only a resulting bearable/livable life.

How does one **make any sense of what happened** to them (get their "WHY" questions answered) and add meaning and purpose (HOPE) to their life so that it results in a more meaningful and fulfilling new life?

As a survivor deals with the emotional crisis they must go through, they must also deal with their confusion as to "WHY" this loss occurred, and possibly, "WHY" it happened in the way it did (totally unexpected, happened at the worst time possible, in the worst way possible, etc.), and other "WHY" questions that arise.

There is no doubt that the more sense a survivor can make about their loss, the easier it is to accept their loss and help eliminate the confusion and help accelerate their healing. I know this book will help you heal quicker and better if I can help you make sense of your loss by helping you answer as many of the "WHY" questions as the Bible provides.

God's Word promises the answers to the question "How do you put meaning and purpose (HOPE) into your NEW LIFE?" It also answers the "WHY" questions.

Are any of these **"WHY"** questions on your mind?

- **Why did a loving God let this happen to me?**
- **Did I do something wrong?**
- **Did my loved one do something wrong?**
- **Was this just happenstance? Or was there a purpose or any meaning in this loss and the hurt I am suffering?**
- **Can I ever really recover and have a peace in my life?**

Yes, I know every survivor would like to make some sense of their loss by finding some value, some good reason for all the confusion, fear, and hurt they are experiencing.

God's Word gives us some very clear reasons why God may have let your loved one's death inflict this pain upon you.

The Bible says that God allows His children to suffer for the following specific reasons:

- **Just to glorify God** because He wants the glory. He is a jealous God and, sometimes He allows confusion, fear, and hurt (human tragedies) so that **"His works"** (miracles, solutions for the better, unbelievable good results) can be shown **just for the purpose of glorifying Him as the one and only God**.
- God promises that the confusion, fear, and hurt that He allows a survivor to suffer will ultimately result in

something **good**, although the one afflicted may never see or know what it is; but God does.

Note: I will provide reasons later why I think "good" things have already happened to you or that are going to happen to you in your healing and growth as a person.

- You have become uniquely qualified as a "wounded warrior" who is now especially qualified to understand and help others through their confusion, fear, and hurt when they have lost a loved one.

- From a Christian perspective, some **lifetime goals have been fulfilled**, and many positive opportunities for your personal growth have been presented.

- The question is: **WHERE ARE YOUR EYES?** **Whose eyes are you looking at your loss through?**

  If you look through **GOD'S** eyes, He is now with His child (your lost loved one).

  Through **YOUR LOVED ONE'S** eyes, they are with their Father God.

  Through **YOUR** eyes, have you seen or are you seeing what your loss has done to improve your relationship with God, discovering who you really are, and finding meaning and purpose in your life?

  Through **OTHER'S** eyes, what have others seen through your testimony for God through your words and actions after this loss, your family's, your church's, the viewings, funeral service, and burial?

Let me develop each one of these biblical answers to see if they make sense to you and aid your healing.

- To **glorify God**, the first answer is that God allows things to happen just so **He is glorified**. At first, that was hard for me to understand and accept because we are taught by the following scriptures to be humble and to be a servant, not to seek glory or any other recognition for our life except to glorify God.

...clothe yourselves, all of you, with humility toward one another, for God opposes the proud but gives grace to the humble. Humble yourselves, therefore, under the mighty hand of God so that at the proper time, He may exalt you. (**1 Peter 5:5–6**)

The greatest among you shall be your servant. Whoever exalts himself will be humbled, but whoever humbles himself shall be exalted. (**Matthew 23:11–12**)

He has brought down the mighty from their thrones and exalted those of humble estate. (**Luke 14:11, Luke 18:14, James 4:10**)

...God opposes the proud but gives grace to the humble... Draw near to God, and He will draw near to you. (**James 4:6**)

...but to the humble, He gives favor. (**Proverbs 3:34**)

I, therefore, a prisoner for the Lord, urge you to walk in a manner worthy of the calling to which you have been called with all humility and gentleness, with patience, bearing with one another in love... (**Ephesians 4:1–3**)

- We, children of God, are to be **humble** in all ways, but God, Himself, does not reflect this in His desire to be glorified. I found it hard to accept the fact that God would allow confusion, fear, and hurt happen to anyone so He would be **glorified**.

- Yet God tells us in the following scriptures that He is the one and only God, and He lets things sometimes just happen so that He is glorified by "His works" being shown and honored.

GOD TELLS US HOW HE FEELS ABOUT RECEIVING GLORY.

I am the Lord; that is my name; my glory I give to no other. (Isaiah 42:8)

...my chosen people, the people I formed for myself that they might declare my praise. (**Isaiah 43:20–21**)

...my glory I will not give to another. (**Isaiah 48:11**)

But you are a chosen race, a royal priesthood, a holy nation, a people for His own possession that **you may proclaim the excellencies of Him** who called you out of darkness into His marvelous light. (**1 Peter 2:9**)

For from Him and through Him and to Him are all things. To Him be glory forever. (**Romans 11:36**)

Sing to the Lord, bless His name, tell of His salvation from day to day.

Declare His glory among the nations, His marvelous works among all the peoples! (**Psalm 96:2–3**)

Splendor and majesty are before Him;
strength and beauty are in His sanctuary.
Ascribe to the Lord, O families of
the peoples, ascribe to the Lord glory and
strength! **(Psalm 96:6–7)**

The **heavens declare the glory of God,
the skies proclaim the work of His hands.**
(**Psalm 19:1–2)**

The Son is the radiance of God's glory.
(Hebrews 1:3, 2 Corinthians 4:6)

And the word became flesh and dwelt among
us, and we have seen His glory, glory as of the
only Son from the Father, full of grace and
truth. **(John 1:14)**

GOD TELLS US ABOUT WHAT HE WANTS FROM HIS CHILDREN.

So whether you eat or drink or whatever you
do, do all to the glory of God. (**1 Corinthians
10:31)**

WHY DID GOD ALLOW THE CRUELTY AND THE INTENSE BEAT-
INGS, THE CRUCIFIXION, AND THE DEATH OF HIS SON, A SIN-
LESS JESUS CHRIST, FOR THE FORGIVENESS OF YOUR SINS?

Remember how Jesus felt about His being crucified so **that
God could be glorified**:

Then Jesus went with them to a place called
Gethsemane, and he said to his disciples,
"Sit here while I go over there and pray." And
taking with him Peter and the two sons of
Zebedee, he began to be sorrowful and trou-

bled. Then he said to them, "My soul is very sorrowful even to death; remain here, and watch with me. And going a little farther, he fell on his face and prayed, saying, "**My Father, if it be possible, let this cup pass from me**; nevertheless, not as I will, but as you will." And he came to the disciples and found them sleeping. And he said to Peter, "So could you not watch with me one hour? Watch and pray that you may not enter temptation. The spirit indeed is willing, but the flesh is weak." Again, for the second time, he went away and prayed, "**My Father, if this cannot pass unless I drink it, your will be done.** And again, he came and found them sleeping, for their eyes were heavy. So leaving them again, he went away and prayed for the **third time**, asking to not have to experience His crucifixion. Then he came to the disciples and said to them, "Sleep and take your rest later on. See, the hour is at hand, and the Son of Man is betrayed into the hands of sinners. Rise, let us be going; see, my betrayer is at hand." (**Matthew 26:36–46, Mark 14:32–42**)

In the garden of Gethsemane, Jesus Christ asked His Father to "take away the cup." Meaning, do not make me suffer the pain and agony of the beatings and the crucifixion and my death and separation from you, Father God, on the cross. Jesus asked three different times because He knew what was going to happen to Him as a man. It was going to hurt, and He really did not want to experience all the excruciating pain as a human.

Then in submission, Jesus prayed:

"Now is my soul troubled. And what shall I say? 'Father save me from this hour?' But for

> this purpose (crucifixion) I have come to this hour. **Father, glorify Your name.**" Then a voice came from Heaven, "**I have glorified it, and I will glorify it again.**" **(John 12:27)**

> When Jesus had spoken these words, he lifted up his eyes to Heaven, and said, "Father, the hour has come; glorify Your Son that the Son may glorify You since you have given him authority over all flesh to give eternal life to all whom you have given him. And this is eternal life that they know You, the only true God, and Jesus Christ whom You have sent. I glorified you on earth having accomplished the work that You gave me to do. And now, Father, glorify me in Your own presence with the glory that I had with you before the world existed." **(John 17:1–5)**

Glorifying God is not a concept that is too hard to accept, is it? When in fact, isn't a Christian's life supposed to be made up of just two things, **glorifying God** and **spreading the good news of the gospel** in all facets of their life?

For a better understanding, let us look at some examples of God allowing people to suffer trials and tribulations just so He would be glorified. Consider the story of the blind man at the well:

> As He passed by, He saw a man blind from birth. And His disciples asked Him, "Rabbi, who sinned, this man or his parents, that he was born blind?" Jesus answered, "It was not that this man sinned or his parents, but that **the works of God might be displayed in him.**" Having said these things, He spit on the ground and made mud with the saliva. Then

He anointed the man's eyes with the mud and said to him, "Go. Wash in the pool of Siloam." So he went and washed and came back seeing. (**John 9:1–7**)

If you tried to figure out why God allowed this blind man to be exposed to his confusion, fear, and hurt so unfairly and unjustly since birth, there does not appear to be any good reason why. But this situation starts to make sense when we read "that the works of God (Jesus's healing miracles) might be displayed "**FOR HIS GLORY**."

Do you think God was glorified here? A man blind for his lifetime, with no apparent reason why he has suffered, is given his sight just so "the works of God" can be shown. Do you think that the people who knew about it thought his God was one to be worshiped and glorified?

LAZARUS

Why did Jesus wait two days after Lazarus died before He went to Lazarus's aid? Martha and Mary complained that Jesus could have kept Lazarus from dying if He just would have gone to be with him right away. Lazarus was a close friend of Jesus. I am sure Jesus loved him; in fact, when Jesus found out Lazarus had died, Jesus wept! (John 11:35) So, why didn't Jesus go and save Lazarus right away?

Jesus told us exactly why:

> ...This illness does not lead to death. **It is for the glory of God so that the Son of God may be glorified through it**. (John 11:4)

> Lazarus had died, and **for your sake I am glad I was not there so that you may believe**. (John 11:14–15)

99

How was God glorified here? Lazarus had died, been prepared for burial, buried, and entombed for a period. Those facts were hard to dispute. So when Jesus called Lazarus and raised him from the grave (a precursor to Jesus's resurrection) and performed such an undisputable miracle, God received the glory because "of His works being shown."

If you lived then, or as you read this now, how do you feel about this God that Jesus was giving glory to with this miracle resurrection of Lazarus?

Question: Relate this situation to your loss and how your loss may be being used to glorify God. How do you think Martha and Mary felt when they had done everything that they could, including going to Jesus and asking Him to go to Lazarus as soon as possible and then watching their brother die and being buried? They were believers. They knew Jesus loved Lazarus and believed Jesus could save Lazarus by performing a life-saving miracle He had done for other people; yet Jesus let Lazarus die. Why?

Admittedly, this was a short time for Martha and Mary to suffer the confusion, fear, and hurt from their loved one's death. However, the sisters could surely understand that what they went through had the end purpose of glorifying God. This miracle resurrection helped them make sense of their suffering and made it more meaningful.

A thought: We will probably never know whether the loss of our loved one glorified God in any way. But we can have the hope that our testimony and actions after our loss and our current grief journey has, is, and will glorify God to fulfill His purpose.

That made sense to me. My loss and my suffering could somehow glorify God and have great meaning and purpose in God's plan and that gives me peace and hope.

EXODUS

My favorite example of God allowing something to happen "so His works can be shown, and He is glorified" is in the book of Exodus. Before I understood Exodus, I always wondered why "God had hardened Pharaoh's heart" was mentioned so many times. In fact, God hardening Pharaoh's heart is mentioned nineteen times.

What we learn from this exchange between God, Moses, Aaron, and Pharaoh is that every time Pharaoh's heart was hardened, he and the people of Egypt suffered devastating consequences. The amazing thing is that Pharaoh observed miraculous signs and suffered ten plagues; yet, he continued to refuse God's direction to free the Hebrews. In fact, he continued to not yield and give glory and recognition to the God of the Hebrews, almost to the total destruction of Egypt.

This was a battle between the Hebrews' God and Pharaoh who claimed he was a god and other gods that the Egyptians worshiped. As you read down through what happened, I'm sure you will agree that somewhere in that process, a significantly battered and wise Pharaoh would have said, "Enough, I want to save myself and my country from total devastation, and I recognize and glorify the Hebrews' God and give the Hebrew's freedom." Why didn't Pharaoh do that? Why did God demand so much glory and make this last so long?

Here is what God said about why He hardened Pharaoh's heart:

> Then the Lord said to Moses, "Go into Pharaoh, for I have hardened his heart and the heart of his servants that I may **show these signs of mine among them** and that you may tell in the hearing of your son and of your grandson how I have dealt harshly with the Egyptians and what **signs I have done**

**among them that you may know that I am
Lord."** (Exodus 10:1–2)

But I will harden Pharaoh's heart, and though
I multiply my signs and wonders in the land
of Egypt, Pharaoh will not listen to you. Then
I will lay my hand on Egypt and bring my
hosts, my people, the children of Israel, out of
the land of Egypt by great acts of judgment.
The Egyptians **shall know that I am Lord**
when I stretch out my hand against Egypt and
bring out the people of Israel from among
them. (**Exodus 7:3–5**)

Thus, sayeth the Lord, the God of the
Hebrews, "Let my people go that they may
serve me. For this time, I will send all my
plagues on you yourself and on your servants
and your people so that you may know that
there is none like me in all the earth. For
by now, I would have put out my hand and
struck you and your people with pestilence,
and you would have been cut off from the
earth. But **for this purpose, I have raised
you up to show you my power** so that my
name may be proclaimed in all the earth."
(**Exodus 9:13**)

Then the Lord said to Moses, "Pharaoh will
not listen to you **that my wonders may be
multiplied in the land of Egypt."** (**Exodus
11:9**)

...nd the Egyptians **shall know that I am
Lord.** (**Exodus 7:5**)

> And I will harden Pharaoh's heart, and he will pursue them, and **I will get glory over Pharaoh and all his host, and the Egyptians shall know that I am the Lord**... (Exodus 14:4)

One cannot help but be impressed with the number of miraculous works God provided to show Pharaoh who He was. The interesting thing is that God hardened Pharaoh's heart so many times to increase and elongate the Egyptian's suffering.

I am providing what happened below to remind us to what length God will go to be glorified and fulfill His promises to His people.

First, Aaron performed three miracles before the elders of the Hebrews in Egypt to convince them God was on their side, and they should go with Moses and Aaron to see Pharaoh.

- His staff turned into a serpent and then back into his staff.
- A portion of water was thrown on the ground, and it turned into blood.
- His hand was inserted into his bosom and came out with flaky skin (like leprosy), and then his hand was healed instantly when inserted back into his bosom.

Note: The elders welcomed Moses and Aaron and observed the miracles. They then pledged that they would go with Moses and Aaron to see Pharaoh. Despite seeing those miracles, they had doubts, and there is no record of them accompanying Moses and Aaron to see Pharaoh. O ye of little faith! Weren't three miracles enough?

MOSES AND AARON VISITED THE PHARAOH:

On Moses and Aaron's first visit, Moses threw his rod down, and it turned into a snake, then when he picked it up, the snake turned back into a rod. They then told Pharaoh that their God said to let His people go and asked that all the Hebrews be allowed just to go into the wilderness for at least seven days to worship their God.

Pharaoh refused and punished the Hebrews by ordering that no straw was to be provided for making bricks. The Hebrews were punished because they still had to produce the same number of bricks per day as they had been providing. The Hebrews then rebelled against Moses; they did not believe God was speaking to Moses because now they were being punished by Pharaoh, and God had not intervened.

In their doubt they said to Moses:

> The Lord look on you and judge, because you have made us stink in the sign of Pharaoh and his servants and have put a sword in their hands to kill us. (**Exodus 5:21**)

> Speaking of faith and human frailty, after all that Moses has seen, he even becomes doubtful and says to God:
> O, Lord why have you done evil to these people? Why did you ever send me? For since I came to Pharaoh to speak in your name, he has done evil to these people, and you have not delivered your people at all. (**Exodus 5:22–23**)

> God tells Moses that He will harden Pharaoh's heart so that He might multiply His signs and wonders in the land of Egypt. (**Exodus 7:3**)

> ...and the Egyptians shall know that I am Lord. (**Exodus 7:5**)

Then Moses and Aaron went to Pharaoh for the **second time**, and Moses touched his rod to the Nile, and the Nile became blood. Aaron then held his arms up, and all the water in containers became blood. In fact, all the water in Egypt became blood.

Note: How extremely damaging this is because all the water becomes undrinkable, and the water dwelling creatures would die. Where did the people find drinkable water? Everyone had to know about this!

On their **third visit**, seven days after the water was turned to blood, frogs appeared everywhere, including inside buildings, etc. Pharaoh requested they be removed, and God showed His power by removing all the frogs, except those in the Nile. Finally, Pharaoh said they could go worship in the desert; but rescinded his order later, and that resulted in

- Aaron's rod being touched to the dust, and lice (vermin) appeared.
- Then insects appeared. Note: All these hardships happened except where the Hebrews were. Pharaoh asked for the insects to stop and to show His power. God removed them, but Pharaoh again refused for the Hebrews to go out of Egypt to the desert to worship their God;
- then pestilence on only the livestock of the Egyptians came, and the livestock died;
- then dust from the kilns that was in the air covered the land, and boils appeared on men and beast.

Question: It is about time for Pharaoh to break and allow about anything, isn't it?

But the Lord hardened the heart of Pharaoh, and he did not listen to them. (**Exodus 9:12**)

- then hail, with thunder and fire intermingled, to devastate man and beast (except the Hebrews);

At this point, Pharaoh's servants were advising him, "Do you not yet understand that Egypt is ruined?" (**Exodus 10:7**)

- then locusts;

But the Lord hardened Pharaoh's heart, and he did not let the people of Israel go. (**Exodus 10:20**)

- then darkness for three days;
- Pharaoh finally said the men could go to the desert to worship but reneged on the request by saying that no women, livestock, or possessions could go;
- God then commanded that the first born of man and livestock would die. (But not Hebrews who put blood on their door for the Passover.) Pharaoh's son then died;
- Pharaoh then finally allowed the Hebrews to leave Egypt. **But Pharaoh did something really weird! He required the Egyptian people to give the Hebrews whatever riches, property, or animals they requested to take with them. (As an interesting aside, the Hebrews were leaving Egypt after more than four hundred years with great wealth just as God promised Abraham would happen in Genesis 15:13–14.)**

Note: God knew back then in the beginning!

...and I will harden Pharaoh's heart, and he will pursue them (to the Red Sea), and I will get glory over Pharaoh and all his host, and

the Egyptians **shall know that I am the Lord**.
(**Exodus 14:4**)

...and the Lord hardened the heart of Pharaoh,
king of Egypt. (**Exodus 14:8**)

- then...

  The waters (of the Red Sea that had parted
  to allow the Hebrews to escape) returned
  and covered the chariots and the horsemen
  (six hundred of the best of Pharaoh's chariots and occupants plus other chariots from
  Egypt); of all the host of Pharaoh that had
  followed them into the Sea, **not one of them
  remained**. (**Exodus 14:28**)

Now you know why God hardened Pharaoh's heart and the
Egyptians experienced so much tragedy and pain. The majesty
and might of the Hebrews' God were shown to the people of
Egypt (and the earth) "by His works" so He could be recognized
as the one and only God and be honored and glorified as He
demanded.

I think this story makes the following points:

- God does not share His glory with anyone or anything.
  He welcomes being seen for who He is and being
  glorified.
- God will sometimes allow His child or children to
  experience trials and tribulations, which causes them
  to suffer confusion, fear, and hurt just so "His works"
  can be shown, and He is recognized for His greatness
  and is glorified. And at least at this time, God's chosen people can see how their suffering has resulted in
  God finally being glorified by them being freed to go to
  their Promised Land (a good result).

- God makes promises to His children. They are promises based on and part of His Eternal Plan for His creation and His people. God is faithful and will fulfill these promises; the fulfillment will be in God's timing, not the sufferer's timing (so they may never see the result of their suffering).

This story illustrates the miraculous machinations He will go through to fulfill His promises and accomplish His Eternal Plan.

Question: Do you have any lingering questions as to whether or not God wants to be glorified? The Exodus story shows us through Scripture that God wants to be recognized as the one and only God and receive glory and to what extent. He will allow "His works" to accomplish the recognition and glory He demands.

What we can learn from this for our healing is that God made a promise to His children as He makes promises to you today that God loved them, He would be their Father God, He would protect, encourage, equip, etc., them, and save them for His own. And that, in His timing, would complete His Eternal Plan for each one's life, including a purpose for each one's life while they are living and at their death.

What a wonderful promise (that God has a plan for each child) to the Hebrews then and to you today. But in the midst of the confusion, fear, and hurt of what happens to us, we ask for an immediate solution and end to our sufferings and want the good and peace that God promises us in His Word. How long must a survivor wait to see the results of what a survivor suffered for? Or will they ever see it in their lifetime?

The Hebrews are a prime example of experiencing confusion, fear, and hurt for a long time while waiting for the answers to the "why" questions. Talk about faith and persistence, I wonder when they started questioning when their confusion, fear, and hurt would be healed? Fifty years? One hundred years? Two hundred years? three hundred? Three hundred and fifty? Four hundred?

The Hebrews' faith was tested for the longest time in history that I am aware of; but the result was what God had promised—the saving and freeing of the whole nation of God's people to ultimately return to their Promised Land.

JOB'S TRIALS AND TRIBULATIONS, THOUGH UNDERSERVED, ENDED UP GLORIFYING GOD.

I think what happened to Job should help reinforce in your mind that one of God's children's suffering can be unjustified and unfair but is allowed by God to fulfill His good and perfect purpose. The child suffers but, in the end, they can accept what happened and heal because it was for God's worthy purpose (here to glorify God).

Talk about unjustified and unfair:

> Job...was blameless and upright, one who feared God and turned away from Evil. (**Job 1:1**)

> In fact, he was so wealthy, and with a family of ten children, that he was,...the greatest of all the people of the east. (**Job 1:3**)

When Satan approached God and challenged God that Job only worshipped God because he was so blessed, God allowed Satan to take away those blessings to prove that Job would still be faithful.

Satan then took away all of Job's children and then all his wealth in just one day.

The significance of Job's loss is sometimes ignored. Recognize that he not only lost all his seven sons and three daughters, but he lost seven thousand sheep, three hundred camels, five hundred yoke of oxen, and five hundred female donkeys.

What did Job do?

> ...he fell on the ground and worshipped. And he said, "Naked I came from my mother's womb, and naked I shall return. The Lord gave, and the Lord has taken away." **Blessed be the name of the Lord. In all this, Job did not sin or charge God with wrong. (Job 1:20–22)**

What was God's response?

> Have you considered my servant Job that there is more like him on the earth, a blameless and upright man, who fears God and turns from evil? **He still holds fast his integrity, although you incited me against him to destroy him without reason. (Job 2:3)**

> God then allows Satan to strike Job with loathsome sores from the sole of his foot to the crown of his head. **(Job 2:7)**

> Then Job's wife said to him, "Do you still hold fast your integrity? **Curse God and die.**" But he said to her, "You speak as one of the foolish women would speak. **Shall we receive good from God, and shall we not receive evil?" In all this, Job did not sin with his lips. (Job 2:9–10)**

Although you know **I am not guilty**, your hands fashioned and made me, and now you have destroyed me altogether. (**Job 10:7–9**)

Though He slay me, I will hope in Him. (**Job 13:15**)

And Job again took up his discourse and said: "As God lives, who has taken away my right, and the Almighty who has made my soul bitter, as long as my breath is in me and the spirit of God is in my nostrils, my lips will not speak falsehood, and my tongue will not utter deceit. Far be it from me to say that you are right: **till I die, I will not put away my integrity from me**. I hold fast my righteousness and will not let it go; my heart does not reproach me for any of my days." (**Job 27:1-6**)

God thunders wondrously with His voice; He does great things that we cannot comprehend. (**Job 37:5**)

Behold, blessed is the one whom God reproves; therefore, **despise not the discipline** of the Almighty. **For He wounds, but He binds up; He shatters, but His hand heals.** (Job 17:18)

Remember the magnitude of what Job has lost, virtually everything. In addition, he had no support. Even God was silent. In fact, **God was silent for the next thirty-five chapters of the Book of Job.** In fact, Job lamented:

He has put my brothers far from me, and those who knew me are wholly estranged from me.

My relatives have failed me, my close friends have forgotten me. (**Job 19:13–14**)

Today also, my complaint is bitter, my hand is heavy on account of my groaning. Oh, that I know where I might find Him. (**Job 23:2–3**)

Behold, I go forward, but He is not there and backward, but I do not perceive Him; on the left hand when He is working, I do not behold Him. He turns to the right hand, but I do not see Him. (**Job 23:8–9**)

I call for help, but there is no justice. (**Job 19:7**)

Job states, "For the thing that I fear comes upon me, and what I dread befalls me. I am not at ease, nor am I quiet; I have no rest, but trouble comes." (**Job 3:25–26**)

Later he states,

He is so miserable he would welcome death. (**Job 6:9**)

Job's three friends then came and stayed with him. They were there for seven days, and they did what one should do to try to comfort someone in distress. They did not say anything and just listened. The friends finally assumed that Job's circumstances were indications that he was in the wrong with God and needed to repent his sin.

Whoops! They broke the cardinal role of "what to say to someone who has met adversity and is suffering!" They did good for seven days and just listened. But then they started to solve Job's situation with their thoughts and ideas. Their main thrust was Job or someone else must have done something wrong for God to let this happen to Job.

But he states,

> "...I have not denied the Words of the Holy One." And he continued to be true to his God. (**Job 6:10**)

Then he said,

> For I know that my Redeemer lives, and at the last, He will stand upon the earth. And after my skin has been thus destroyed, yet in my flesh I shall see God who I should see for myself, and my eyes shall behold and not another. (**Job 19:25–27**)

Job affirmed,

> But He knows the way that I take; when he has tried me, I shall come out as gold. My foot has held fast to His steps; I have kept His way and have not turned aside. I have not departed from the commandments of His lips; I **have treasured the words of His mouth** more than my portion of food. (**Job 23:10**)

> Behold, the fear of the Lord that is wisdom, and to turn away from evil is understanding. (**Job 28:28**)

What faith in the midst of all this unfairness he is showing! Then God finally spoke to Job, and **Job repented by saying something very meaningful**.

> Then Job answered the Lord and said, "I know that you can do all things, and that no purpose of yours can be thwarted." (**Job 42:1–2**)

> ...Therefore, **I have uttered what I did not understand, things too wonderful for me, which I did not know.** (Job 42:3)

> I had heard of you by the hearing of the ear, **but now my eye sees you**. (Job 42:5)

I identified with Job in that I have **heard**, read, and studied about God and thought I understood God's character and had faith in Him. But in addition, I thought, acted, and **uttered what I did not understand, things too wonderful for me, which I did not really know.**

Job said finally, "Now **my eyes see you**" (**Job 42:5**). I think God was revealing the highest standard for us to attain to have the relationship He wants to have with us. **Each one of us should strive to really "see" God.** Seeing entails knowing God's character ultimately through knowing His scripture and, more importantly, **experiencing, receiving, and giving His love and the results**. In other words, LIVE IT! EXPERIENCE IT! And SEE HIM!

Job was never told why he was experiencing these hardships. Yet he stayed steadfast in his love for and worship of God no matter the pain and suffering he experienced. When Job's testing was finished, the Lord returned to him twice as much of material wealth as he had before (i.e., fourteen thousand sheep, six hundred camels, one thousand yoke of oxen, and one thousand female donkeys). He was also blessed with a new family of sons and daughters. Scripture then reports that Job later died an old man and full of days.

How would you react if you had lost all your children and all your possessions then was stricken with sores all over your body **when there is no apparent reason why**? How are you reacting to your loss, a loss with, perhaps, no reason why that is apparent to you?

Will your confusion, fear, and hurt pull you away from a life lived with God and His love and promises?

So the Bible tells us that it is possible that part or all the meaning and purpose for what happened to you could be just for the **ultimate glorification of God—glorification** which He desires as shown by the stories about the blind beggar, Lazarus, the Exodus, and Job.

The tendency is for a survivor, in their emotional state, not to be able to see that their loss could be glorifying God.

But there is great hope that **God has been recognized and glorified in different ways** by your loss. For example:

- upon the death of your loved one, their loved ones, friends, and acquaintances that could be faced with the reality of death and its unknowns that will someday affect their life. Consequently, your loved one's death may lead others to seek the security and love of God while they are living;
- by your conduct or someone's conduct glorifying God at the visitations, the funeral service or at the burial service;
- by your life and testimony in your actions in your healing process.

So I believe that the Bible tells us that there can be comfort in knowing that no matter how confusing, with no apparent reason for or results from what happened to you, and no matter how unjustified and unfair it seems to be, God could have allowed your loss just for His glorification.

Ask the Hebrews enslaved for four hundred years in Egypt and waiting to be freed by their God. Ask Job. Ask the blind man at the well. Ask Lazarus. Was there CONFUSION, FEAR and HURT? YES! Did the suffering seem unfair? Yes. Did there seem to be any meaning or purpose in their suffering? No.

But did their suffering ultimately result in God getting the glory He purposed? Yes!

GOD ALLOWS THINGS TO HAPPEN FOR GOOD.

The second reason that could help make sense of your loss and suffering is that Scripture says,

> And we know that for those who love God,
> all things work together for GOOD for those
> who are called according to His purpose.
> **(Romans 8:28)**

Yes, it says all things, and it says **for good!**

Would your loss make more sense and be more acceptable if you knew that what you are going through has already or will result in something good? (Maybe not in the specific good you would desire but result in something good God desires.)

The Bible reinforces God's love for you when God states,

> **For I know the plans I have for you,....plans**
> **for your welfare and not for evil to give you**
> **a future and hope. (Jeremiah 29:11)**

Yes, God controls all things and allowed your loss to happen to you; but His word says that **all** things happen for good within His eternal purpose.

This good gives a peace in one's life; it gives hope in one's life to know their suffering, and grief will result in a good result someday, somehow, somewhere. The survivor may never see or experience that good, or they may get to see and experience that good; but either way, they can know that God has an Eternal Plan, and their **suffering will result in some good result as planned by God** somehow and sometime as promised.

That is not too unbelievable, is it? There are many good results that have been experienced from the loss of a loved one. In fact, I would challenge you to evaluate whether or not some of these good things have happened or are happening to you right now.

CONSIDER SOME OF THE GOOD RESULTS POSSIBLY HAPPENING TO YOU IN YOUR HEALING PROCESS RIGHT NOW.

- Your desire for a closer relationship with God
- Having a greater relationship and appreciation for one's family and other people around you
- An increased desire to put your life in order—financial, relationships, physical, spiritual
- An increased desire to know what the Bible says
- A desire to understand yourself, to ask "who am I," to help you refine who you are as a person
- A desire to find what your purpose is in life, including what God's purpose for you is
- Having an opportunity to start all or various facets of your life anew

How realistic are the above possible good results happening to you in your life in your healing right now? Are you starting to experience any of the above-mentioned positive growth in who you are and are becoming as mentioned above?

I want to compare what has happened to you to the story of Joseph. It is, to me, the best example of a good result coming out of much unfairness, confusion, fear, and hurt.

Joseph told his brothers,

> You meant evil against me, but God meant it for good. (**Genesis 50:20**)

This is one little sentence but is representative of fourteen years of unfairness and suffering for Joseph. In the beginning,

Joseph seemed to be a man of God and be blessed with visitations and visions from God; but until the final outcome, it was hard to see why God allowed him to suffer.

Notice the **good** that came out of his suffering was very significant, it was the saving of the Hebrew nation by moving Joseph's father, Jacob, and seventy other family members and other chosen people from Canaan to Egypt.

The importance of their moving to Egypt was that there had been two years of famine in Canaan where Jacob and God's chosen people lived. There was five more years of famine to go, which most likely would have annihilated Jacob and God's chosen people.

God set up the saving of His chosen people (a good result) through a lot of unfair confusion, fear, and hurt levied on just one boy/man, Joseph.

Compare your situation, your questions, and your doubts from what has happened to you to the questions and doubts Joseph must have felt about what happened to him. Joseph had the same heavy testing of his belief in and reliance on God that you have had. Yet Joseph, through all His affliction, persevered and apparently continued doing his best to be faithful and to glorify his God. His continuance of giving his best effort was evidenced by his advancing so rapidly in any new position he had. But no matter how he bettered himself, unfairness would happen again, putting him in even worse conditions.

THE STORY OF JOSEPH

Before Joseph was seventeen years old, he had a close relationship with God. In fact, Joseph had visitations and visions from God. One vision he told his brothers about was that he saw his brothers kneeling before him on three different occasions.

This upset his brothers and combined with the fact that Joseph was the favorite of his father, the brothers plotted to kill him. First, they threw him into a pit and left him to die. Then they decided they would make some money on his life, so they took him out of the pit and sold him as a slave to someone in a caravan going to Egypt. The brothers then returned Joseph's coat of many colors with blood stains on it to their father and told him Joseph was dead.

I am using this story to point out some important lessons for your healing:

- I pointed out that Scripture says that everything happens for good if it is in God's purposes. We will test that with this story!
- Observe how Joseph's life gyrates up and down and seems so very unfair.
  Especially unfair when he seemed to have a close relationship with God and had not forsaken his relationship with God. So why did God let this happen to him? He suffered many hurts without any indication that he deserved any of them. He had remained faithful to God. All the confusion, fear, and hurt was heaped upon Joseph for no apparent reason. I am sure he could not figure out why all this was happening to him, but he surely would like to know. I promise, he would find out the good at the end, as will you.
- Compare this story and Joseph's plight to your situation, the unfairness and no clear explanation as to why this happened to you and why you are suffering, no clear good result foreseeable now or in the future but a promise from God that He has an Eternal Plan for His children and for you individually where things will happen in our life, even bad things, for the ultimate good that He wants to happen. (Although the sufferer may never know the good or see it.)

Let us look at Joseph's life and see what happened:

- After being betrayed by his own brothers and left to die, he was then retrieved from a pit and sold into slavery. Joseph was then sold to an Egyptian captain of the guard in Pharaoh's army named Potiphar. Scripture says that "the Lord was with Joseph (why wasn't He with him at the pit and later being sold into slavery?), and he became a successful man (Genesis 39:2). And "his master saw that the Lord was with him and that the Lord caused all that he did to succeed in his hands" (Genesis 39:3). So Joseph was made head of everything Potiphar had.

Unfortunately, Potiphar's wife was attracted to Joseph, who was very handsome, and she wanted to have relations with him. He refused and she then lied and accused him of trying to molest her. Potiphar responded and put Joseph in a prison where only Pharaoh's personal prisoners were confined.

Let me ask you right here, how are you feeling about your situation, confusion, fear, hurt, and unfairness? How do you think Joseph felt? Abandoned by his brothers, sold as a slave by his own brothers, apparently blessed by God and advanced to head of Potiphar's house, and then falsely accused and put in prison; all this without any apparent reason—why was God letting this happen to Joseph?

- In prison, "The Lord was with Joseph and showed him steadfast love and gave him favor in sight of the keeper of the prison. And the keeper of the prison put Joseph in charge of all of the prisoners who were in the prison. Whatever was done there, he was the one who did it" (Genesis 39:21–22).

  Notice the significance of the fact that this was a prison where Pharaoh's personal prisoners were confined. Pharaoh sent his cupbearer (who made sure Pharaoh was not poisoned) and his baker to prison. Later they each had a dream, and Joseph interpreted what the dreams meant.

The cupbearer dreamed of a vine with three branches. As soon as it budded its blossoms burst forth and the cluster ripened into grapes, Pharaoh's cup was in the cupbearer's hand, he pressed the grapes in the cup and put the cup in Pharaoh's hand. Joseph interpreted that in three days. The cupbearer would be released and become Pharaoh's cupbearer again.

As Joseph predicted, in three days, the cupbearer was reinstated as Pharaoh's cupbearer.

Unfortunately for the baker, his dream meant that in three days, he would be beheaded, and that happened too.

Two years later, around the thirteenth year Joseph was in prison, Pharaoh had two different dreams that his seers could not interpret. The cupbearer remembered Joseph's ability to interpret dreams and recommended him to Pharaoh. Joseph told Pharaoh that God was telling him what God was going to do. There would be seven years of great prosperity, and then seven years of severe famine, and someone wise should be put in charge of storing up and saving in the good years and oversee preparation for the famine that will be all over the earth in the seven bad years.

Pharaoh was so impressed that he appointed Joseph and said, "You shall be over my house, and my people shall order themselves as you command" (**Genesis 41:38–40**).

Joseph was made the second most powerful man in Egypt at age thirty.

- Seven good years passed and two years into the famine, which indeed had affected all the earth, including Canaan, Joseph's father, Jacob, sent nine of his brothers to Egypt to purchase grain.

They entered the presence of the official who sold the grain, Joseph. They did not recognize him and bowed before him with their faces to the ground.

Note: As a matter of fact, the dream Joseph told his brothers about was fulfilled two more times as his brothers visited two more times and kneeled before him, still not recognizing him.

Finally, Joseph identified himself and tells them that there is five more years of famine, starvation, and death coming, and they should go and get Jacob and his household and bring them to Egypt.

In fact, Pharaoh sent Jacob a message to bring his household (people) and have no concerns for your goods; for the best of all of Egypt is yours (**Genesis 45:18–20**).

God also said to Jacob,

> ...do not be afraid to go down to Egypt, for there I will make you into a great nation. I myself will go down with you to Egypt, and I will also bring you up again (back to Canaan, the Promised Land). (**Genesis 46:3-4**)

Does this story reinforce that good can come out of much confusion, fear, and hurt? Joseph's journey of grief ended in the monumental result of saving the whole Jewish nation that God promised was His, and He would protect. Notice the ups and downs of Joseph's journey (like yours), with no apparent reason why they were happening. But most of all, notice the good results in the saving of God's promised peoples' lives and providing them a safe place to live.

Remember what Joseph said to his brothers when the "good" results appeared.

> As for you, you meant evil against me but God meant it for good, to bring it about that many people should be kept alive, as they are today. (**Genesis 50:20**)

>...to preserve for you a remnant on the earth
>and to keep alive for you many survivors. So
>it was not you who sent me here. (**Genesis
>45:7–8**)

>...you meant evil against me, but God meant
>it for good. (**Genesis 50:20**)

There is a wonderful peace in believing that God has promised a good result (although sometimes you may never see it, or you may never feel it). Thus, there could be meaning and purpose (an ultimate good or more than one good result) in your loved one's loss, and why your confusion, fear, and hurt has meaning.

To me, God said, "All things happen for good." He meant it; He commands that result. It is His purpose, and something worthy and good will come out of what He allowed to happen to me and you.

Personally, I have experienced much good from the loss of my wife. I have had my faith in God sorely tested, causing me to read many books, and the Bible, to find out what I should know about being a Christian. I have a much closer relationship with my Father, God. I could start my grief healing by stopping the denial of my wife's death and accept that it happened, and her death was for a good purpose and/or for glorifying God. I have a greater appreciation of my need to serve others and work at it and of my need for the support of my family and other people outside of my family.

Thank You, Lord, that I know your love for me, how you pursued me, and now that I know more about Your character. I have hope that gives me Your peace.

To help you make sense of the above, I hope you can see that your loss could end up **glorifying God** and/or could result in the **good** that God promises, ending in a worthwhile result worth the confusion, fear, and hurt experienced.

WHAT DOES THE BIBLE SAY ABOUT WHAT "GOOD" RESULTS GOD PROMISES WILL COME FROM THE TRAGEDY LIKE YOU ARE GOING THROUGH?

God tells us that even though He loves us, He will allow hardships in our life.

> For the Lord will not cast off forever, but though He causes grief, He will have compassion according to the abundance of His steadfast love. (**Lamentations 3:31–33**)

> (About God bringing trials and tribulations to His own son, Jesus) Yet it was the will of the Lord to crush him; he has put him to grief; (And what good came out of this? The saving and salvation of all sinners for the rest of time!) (**Isaiah 53:10**)

> Shall we receive good from God. Also, shall we not receive evil? (**Job 2:10**)

> I have said these things to you that in me you may have peace. In the world, you will have tribulation. But take heart, I have overcome the world. (**John 16:33**)

Yes, you will have trials and tribulations, but His Word is very clear about ultimately turning suffering and hardship into a triumph and hope.

> We also rejoice in our **sufferings** because we know that suffering produces **endurance**, and **endurance** produces **character**, and **character** produces hope. (**Romans 5:3–5**)

124

Count it all **joy**, my brothers, when you meet trials of various kinds, for you know that the testing of your faith produces **steadfastness**. And let steadfastness have its full effect that you may be **perfect** and **complete, lacking in nothing.** (James 1:2-4)

For this light, momentary affliction is preparing us for an eternal weight of glory beyond all comparison... (**2 Corinthians 4:17–18**)

In this you rejoice even now for a while if necessary, you have been grieved by various trials so that the total genuineness of your faith—more precious than gold that perishes though it is tested by fire—may be found to result in praise and glory and honor. (**1 Peter 1:6**)

Blessed is that man who remains STEADFAST UNDER TRIAL, for when he has stood the test, he will receive the crown of life, which God has promised to those who love Him. (**James 1:12**)

Those who sow in tears will reap with songs of joy. (**Psalm 126:5**)

Blessed are those who **mourn**, for they shall be **comforted**. (**Matthew 5:4**)

The Lord has comforted His people and will have compassion upon them in their sorrow. (**Isaiah 49:13**)

I consider that our **present sufferings** are not worth comparing with the glory that will be revealed to us. (**Romans 8:18**)

The Lord will be your everlasting light, and your days of mourning shall be ended. (Isaiah 60:20)

Weeping may tarry for the night, but **joy** comes with the morning. (**Psalm 30:5**)

You have turned for me my **mourning into dancing** and clothed me with **gladness**. (**Psalm 30:11**)

Men are not cast off by the Lord forever. Though He brings **grief**, He will show **compassion**, so great is His unfailing love. For He does not willingly bring affliction or grief to the children of men. (**Lamentations 3:31–33**)

FROM TRAGEDY TO TRIUMPH

Do not miss what you have just read! What wonderful promises!—the promise of triumphs out of the tragedies we are experiencing as survivors, faith in the goodness of God and patience—God teaches it all through the Bible! Now is the time we must listen and learn how God works. He promises good coming out of your experience. We are not sure when that good will come or you will ever see it, but you must have faith and patience.

I have prepared a summary of the scriptures you just read showing your situation, the results, and the wonderful **future promises of good** that God gives us, resulting from the confusion, fear, and hurt you are experiencing.

Keep these promises and a survivor's prayer, I will give you later, in front of you every morning to start off the day. There is meaning in your suffering, and most importantly, there is **HOPE** for the future!

The following chart, Tragedy to Triumph, was created to highlight the scriptures you have just read. It highlights the various situations a survivor might experience and the resulting phases of personal growth and healing a survivor would experience, then the final various **good** results the scriptures promise.

TRAGEDY TO TRIUMPH

YOUR SITUATION	GROWTH & HEALING	FUTURE PROMISE OF A GOOD RESULT
SUFFERING Romans 5:3–5	PERSEVERANCE CHARACTER	HOPE
TRIALS James 1:2–4	TESTING OF FAITH	PERFECT NOT LACK ANYTHING
TROUBLES 2 Corinthians 4:17–18	ONLY TEMPORARY	ETERNAL. GLORY
GRIEF/TRIALS 1 Peter 1:6	TESTING OF FAITH BECOME GENUINE	PRAISE/GLORY/ HONOR
TRIALS James 1:12	STEADFASTNESS PERSEVERANCE	CROWN OF LIFE

TEARS		
Psalm 126:5	GOD'S COMPASSION	SONGS OF JOY

MOURN		
Matthew 5:4	GOD'S COMFORTING	COMFORTED SORROW
Isaiah 49:13	GOD'S COMPASSION	COMFORTED SUFFERINGS
Romans 8:18	GOD'S COMPASSION	GLORY MOURNING
Isaiah 60:20	GOD'S COMPASSION	MOURNING WILL END WEEPING
Psalm 30:5	GOD'S COMPASSION	JOY COMES IN THE MORNING MOURNING
Psalm 30:11	GOD'S COMPASSION	GLADNESS GRIEF
Lamentations 3:31–33	GOD'S COMPASSION	PEACE TROUBLES
2 Corinthians 1:4–7	GOD'S COMFORT	MORE ABLE TO COMFORT OTHERS

My favorite part of this chart is that it promises that I have a future as a person because I will be changed, molded, and improved as I learn **perseverance** and **steadfastness**.

Steadfastness will give me **character** (character means striving to obtain the character of God and Jesus) and the above will give me hope. **No matter what happened, I can make it with hope, and so can you.**

God may allow tragedy to come into one's life, but He promises that it will turn into triumph.

So I hope I have shown you how you are seen through God's eyes and shown you the meaningful future (good for you and, hopefully, good for others) you have been promised from experiencing your loss. Have faith and be patient.

GOD HAS DEFINITELY GIVEN YOU ONE GOOD NEW PURPOSE IN LIFE ALREADY

Another extremely meaningful result of your loss is that you have become a "wounded healer." You have been prepared and are now qualified to comfort others who have lost a loved one.

> Who comforts us in all our afflictions so that we may be able to comfort those who are in any affliction with the comfort with which we ourselves are comforted by God. (**2 Corinthians 1:4**)

> Bear one another's burdens, and so fulfill the law of Christ. (**Galatians 6:2**)

> If one member suffers, all suffer together. (**1 Corinthians 12:26**)

Most survivors are surprised by their new opportunity to be helpful to someone else. They do not feel qualified to help others because of their own confusion and painful condition; but they are valuable to others who have lost a loved one.

Because of your loss, you are the one who someone who has lost a loved one can talk to and be trusted to tell you how they are feeling about **their** loss and the hurt and confusion they are experiencing. A survivor is trustworthy, and their greatest value to other survivors is that they will understand the confusing situation they are in and have empathy for them. A survivor becomes a fellow wounded sister or brother.

It has been mentioned by participants to me many times in our program that as soon as they mention the loss of their loved one, so many people opened up and started talking about their pain or a lost loved one too. However you are feeling, wherever you are in your healing process, you are invaluable to them just to have a chance to talk about their situation to you no matter whether you think you know enough to help or how you are feeling. Just the chance to talk about their loss is very important and should be pursued. Just think how much more helpful you can be when you are advanced in your healing process!

This trustworthiness carries over to any meeting of survivors. Just being together and sharing is extremely therapeutic. **It is the best activity you could pursue!** Who will better understand if you talk or do not talk or if you are moody or downright angry or sad? They rally around each other after the meeting, sharing even more between themselves.

Do not underestimate your importance in your ability to help other survivors!

THERE ARE SOME OTHER GOOD RESULTS IF ONE ASKS, "WHERE ARE YOUR EYES?" WHOSE EYES ARE WE LOOKING AT THIS LOSS THROUGH?

What does your loss look like through God's eyes, your loved one's eyes, your eyes, and other people's eyes?

If you look at your loss through **GOD'S EYES**, your loved one is with Him immediately, holy and without blemish because of Christ's sacrifice. Read **Ephesians 1:4–12**.

God has gained because His heart's desire is to have His children with Him. Read **John 17:24**.

Through your **LOVED ONE'S EYES**, your loved one's life goal as a Christian was to, ultimately, be in Heaven with their

Father for eternity if their lives have born witness to Jesus. They have entered His presence and are with the saints and martyrs of the Bible, holy and without blemish. Read **Revelations 6:9–11**.

Paul wanted this as he said,

> For me to live is Christ, and to die is gain...
> My desire is to depart and be with Christ, for
> that is far better. (**Philippians 1:21–23**)

Paul also shared with the Corinthians:

> For we know that if the tent that is our earthly
> home is destroyed, we have a building from
> God, a house not made with hands, eternal
> in the heavens. For in this tent we groan,
> longing to put on our heavenly dwelling. (**2
> Corinthians 5:1–2**)

> ...we would rather be away from the body and
> at home with the Lord. (**2 Corinthians 5:8**)

Also, your loved one is no longer subject to life's travails. In contrast, you are experiencing those travails right now.

What do you see through **YOUR EYES**? At first not much because you are affected by just trying to deal with the several crises in your life (i.e., dealing with your emotions and the stressful everyday demands and happenings in your life). But as you heal, your eyes start to see some results or changes in your life, hopefully for the better.

Have any of these "good" things happened to you yet?

- You desire a closer relationship with God.
- You are starting to rely on God's promises and His protection.

- You have an increased desire to put your life in order: financial, relationships, physical, spiritual.
- You have an increased appreciation of family and other people.
- You desire to find meaning in your loved one's death and the future meaning and purpose of your life, seeking who am I?
- You are a wounded healer, experiencing God's comfort and being able to, in turn, give comfort to other survivors (2 Corinthians 1:4–7).

Remember, you are important to God. God wants to have a strong, close relationship with you. God wants all the above good results to happen. They will all bring you closer to the peace in life that you are seeking.

Looking through the EYES OF OTHERS, when looking at your loss through the eyes of others, there is an opportunity to introduce them to God. Others are watching you and waiting to see the outcome of your loss.

I discussed earlier that we do not know what "other people's eyes" have seen and what they have heard since you have lost your loved one. We do not know if God has been newly introduced, if He has been glorified in some way or something "good" has happened; but it could have happened or will happen.

If you heal and live a new fulfilled life with meaning and purpose and attribute such to the reasons I have presented in this book (the Balm of Jesus), then God's love and provisions receive credit for your new life, and God is glorified.

Oh, how the angels must celebrate and sing when God is glorified!

That should be enough to motivate you to live a new fulfilled life. What a wonderful life experience you will have living within God's purpose for you as a goal!

"Where are your eyes?" I hope you will agree, when you are ready to consider the above, that when you look at your loss from God's, your loved ones', your, and others' eyes that some "good" and positive results can make your loss make sense and have meaning and purpose.

Sometimes another question a survivor has is, Why is this happening to me? Did I do something wrong, or did somebody else do something wrong, and we are being punished?

There is no way I can give you any way to determine if someone has done something wrong. If so, God's plan will work that out with them. But remember, even if you or someone else did something wrong, you must heal and deal with God's plan for you. Remember that sometimes, nobody is at fault. God sometimes allows things or makes things happen just so He is glorified. Remember the blind man at the well, the Exodus, Job, or Lazarus? None of them did anything wrong, but a good result came from a lifetime of blindness, the trauma of dying and being entombed and resurrected, and Job's devastating losses and suffering for a period of time.

God wants to be recognized and glorified. Perhaps He allowed your loss and is watching your life intended to glorify Him.

At other times, God allows things to happen because His plan is for them to result in something good.

SUMMARY

So there you have it, the heart of the book. The reasons why your life today can start healing and develop into the meaningful and fulfilled life it can be.

Please remember that my understanding is that unless you can find some meaning and/or purpose in your loss, the eternal questions of "why did this happen to me?" will continue without any closure or ending point. With closure and acceptance, a survivor can get on with their new life and **recover life instead of spending life recovering**.

God allows things to happen, some good and some bad. We just reviewed that God promises that all things that happen are for good for those who are in a relationship with Him and as part of His Eternal Plan (not your personal plan or what you want to happen). If you can reinforce or renew your mind right here and accept that the end result of your experience will be God's plan "for good" or will result in His glorification, then you can move forward relieved of wondering and armed with that belief and hope that there was meaning and purpose in the death of your loved one!

Yes, just keep repeating, "I don't know why my loved one died, but I accept that it happened, and I am relying on the promise that my Father God gives me that my loss will result in glorifying Him and/or will result in something good. I hope to see it, but I may never see it in my lifetime. But I have a peace that there was meaning and purpose in my loved one's death. The confusion, fear, and hurt that I am experiencing has a reason and that is important to me."

So your next new life question then is "**why am I still here?**" God has made that very clear (and I hope I made it clear in the section on how much God loves you and what His promises are for you). You are still here for a purpose. Finding that purpose will keep you from ending up with just a bearable/livable life (spending life recovering) and provide you with the meaningful and fulfilled life I want for you (recover life).

THE BALM OF CHRIST

Please accept and use my term *the balm of Christ* for making the loss of your loved one able to be acceptable in your eyes. God's love and the promises we have received in His Word are the balm of Christ, the healing reasons that give the loss of your loved one meaning and purpose (will result in glorifying God and/or something good somehow and somewhere per God's Word).

What is required is the renewing of your mind to accept that God's good purposes will result from what has happened and what will happen in your new life.

> Do not be conformed to this world, but be transformed by the **renewal of your mind** that by testing, you may discern what is the will of God, what is good and acceptable and perfect. (**Romans 12:2**)

> That the God of our Lord Jesus Crist, the Father of glory, may give you the spirit of wisdom and a revelation in the knowledge of Him, **having the eyes of your hearts enlightened, that you may know what is the hope to which He has called you, what are the riches of His glorious inheritance in the saints.** (**Ephesians 1:17–18**)

Accepting, in your eyes, what has happened to you is the start of healing. But you still must deal with your current and future new life or an everyday basis. The confusion, fear, and hurt will still be there, but its intensity and the length of time it lasts is directly related to one's personal relationship with Jesus. Finding God's purpose in your new life allows you to continue to grow in faith and hope—the recovery of life that we all so want, all that and peace resulting from the balm of Christ.

In fact, in my opinion, these are the same possible reasons answering why God allows the confusion, fear, and hurt in one's life that comes from divorce, health problems, bankruptcy, family problems, losing one's job, and other human tragedies.

DOES GOD REALLY HAVE AN ETERNAL PLAN?— REALITY OR MYTH

I have stated that if you want to heal and have a new life that is meaningful and fulfilled that you recognize the fact that the Bible says that you can take comfort and have hope in the fact that there was meaning and purpose in what happened to you because it is part of God's Eternal Plan. Part of His plan is that some things happen to either **glorify** Him directly (such as the blind beggar at the well or Job's life or Lazarus's resurrection story, the Exodus story, or Jesus's and the disciples' miracles) or allows something to happen to one of His children that causes confusion, fear, and hurt but results, ultimately, in something happening that is a **good result**.

If the reasons above make sense as to why my loved one's loss had meaning and purpose (God's purpose) in my past life, then what is going to help me find hope, meaning, and purpose in my future new life?

God's Word says that what happened to you in the past, what is happening to you now, and what happens in your new life is part of God's Eternal Plan for you.

Does God really have an Eternal Plan for all the earth and its inhabitants and, particularly, you individually?

I want to tell you two stories from the Bible that surely illustrate that He does have an Eternal Plan, and He will go to great lengths over long periods of time to complete it.

For brevity, let me summarize how the **story of Joseph's life** and the **exodus of the Israelites from Egypt** illustrates that **God had a plan,** He made a promise to fulfill His plan, and notice the confusion, fear, and hurt He allowed to happen to complete His plan.

THE STORY OF JOSEPH

GOD'S PROMISE to His chosen people of the Abraham, Isaac, and Jacob lineage:

A long time ago, God promised Abraham that his lineage of people (Isaac's then Jacob's) would be God's chosen people, and they would fellowship with Him and be blessed and be given their own holy land to live in someday (Canaan).

GOD'S PLAN

So you understand the significance of what Joseph went through and the resulting "**GOOD**" result, you need to know that at the time of this story, a world famine occurred that was threatening to starve and annihilate God's chosen people (Abraham's lineage) living in Canaan at that time.

Jacob's lineage had to be saved from a world famine by leaving Canaan and going to Egypt where there was food.

How did God make that happen? How did God keep His chosen people from being annihilated by a famine?

137

THE LIFE OF JOSEPH—WHAT A STORY!

Joseph was seventeen years old. He was Jacob's second youngest son, one of twelve sons. He had a dream that someday his brothers would kneel at his feet. He told his brothers about his dream. This, and the additional fact that Joseph seemed to be the favorite son of Jacob, made them angry enough to throw him down into a pit to die. They reconsidered and got him out of the pit and sold him into slavery where he was taken to Egypt.

He was sold into slavery to an Egyptian officer. He performed his slave's tasks so well that he was soon put in charge of the whole Egyptian officer's household. The officer's wife tried to seduce him, and he refused. She then lied and said he assaulted her, so Joseph, quite unfairly, was then sent to prison where he was to spend the next fourteen years.

He performed so well in prison that he was quickly promoted to running the prison. While in prison, he interpreted the dreams of two fellow prisoners, a baker, and a cupbearer for the pharaoh of Egypt. Joseph's interpretation for both came true very shortly, the cupbearer went back into the service of Pharaoh, and the baker soon died.

Two years passed, and Pharaoh had a dream that his seers could not interpret. The cupbearer remembered Joseph, and he was called from prison. Joseph told Pharaoh that the dreams meant there would be seven years of good times and plenty and then seven years of famine.

Pharaoh believed Joseph and took him into his household. Joseph was so efficient that, ultimately, he **became second only to Pharaoh in authority over all of Egypt**.

So Joseph had Pharaoh's people accumulate provisions over the good years and was well stocked when the famine did come. The famine was so severe and widespread it even reached where Jacob and his family were located in Canaan. Jacob sent different sons to find provisions on a series of trips to Egypt. The sons met with Joseph each time but did not recognize him.

(Note: the sons kneeled at Joseph's feet three different times, which fulfilled Joseph's dreams.)

After two years into the famine and after the son's visits, Joseph finally reveals himself to his brothers and persuaded Pharaoh to invite Jacob and all his family to Egypt because of the famine. Jacob and his family consisted of seventy plus people who movde to Egypt and safety. (Note: it is interesting to note that Jacob's family was moved to the best grazing land in Egypt because the Egyptians were not shepherds and did not use this valuable grazing land.)

So I ask you, do you think God had a plan (a promised heritage to Abraham's seed to be God's chosen people and to continue in existence—saved from the famine—until they are redelivered to their Promised Holy Land home, Canaan)? Notice the machinations God went through to get Joseph to Egypt and, ultimately, becomes the leader of Egypt to be able to protect Jacob and his lineage from the famine.

God had a plan for **good**; He made a promise, and in His timing, He made it happen!

Since this is written for you as a survivor, I also want you to identify with Joseph and what he must have thought and wondered while experiencing all of these good and bad things that happened to him for no apparent good reason.

Joseph's view is not very attractive (or clear) at first— betrayed by your brothers, thrown in a pit to die, and then sold as a slave, then taken to Egypt and sold as a slave there, then put in prison for fourteen years because of a woman's lies.

Joseph also had good and encouraging times—becoming the head of the officer of the guard's household and becoming the head of the prison he was in, then going directly from prison to becoming the second most powerful man in Egypt.

What is important is to recognize that Joseph's ups and downs ultimately resulted in saving the lives of his whole family (God's chosen people), including those brothers who betrayed him who he ultimately forgave.

It took a lot of faith and patience to weather the storms of Joseph's ups and downs, but the result was very good! In fact, Joseph told his brothers:

> I am your brother, Joseph, whom you sold into Egypt. And now do not be distressed or angry with yourselves because you sold me here, for **God sent me before you to preserve life**. (**Genesis 45:4–5**)

> And God sent me before you to preserve a remnant on earth and to keep alive for you many survivors. So **it was not you who sent me here but God**. (**Genesis 45:7**)

> And to be very clear, he said: as for you, you meant evil against me, **but God meant it for good** to bring it about that many people should be kept alive as they are today. (**Genesis 50:20**)

GOD'S PLAN FOR HIS CHOSEN PEOPLE CONTINUES 430 YEARS LATER IN THE EXODUS—A LONG WAIT AND A LOT OF SUFFERING FOR FINALLY A GOOD RESULT

After being brought to Egypt, the Israelites had stayed in Egypt 430 years. But God's children had become slaves in Egypt. What happened to God's plan and promise to deliver Abraham's seed to the Promised Holy Land? One could legitimately ask where God has been for all those years?

Finally, it became time for the freeing of His people and their delivery to their Promised Land.

I am telling you this story because I think it parallels your experience, and if it has the significance to you as it does to me, it will confirm God's good character and how He allows things to happen to His children that seem to be unjustified and unfair that cause confusion, fear, and hurt but result in a God-purposed good result (freedom from slavery and their ultimate delivery to the Promised Land).

You are suffering, confused, fearful, and hurting. Compare that to the Israelites who were promised they were God's chosen people, and they would have a homeland someday, and yet they were slaves in a foreign land and had been for **hundreds of years**. Why was God silent? Why were they put in this position of slavery, confusion, fear, and hurt amidst all the promises made to them?

Notice the different parts of God's Eternal Plan that caused confusion, fear, and hurt among different people independently of each other. Yet all of their trials and tribulations culminated in God's good purpose—for example, the showing of miracles to the elders of the Israelites to alleviate their fears; God having allowed the enslavement and persecution of the Israelites; the enslaved Israelite's subsequent viewing of the plagues and maladies placed on Egypt; the miraculous cloud in the sky protecting them as they left Egypt; the parting of the Red Sea and the provision of manna to eat; and the protective cloud, day and night, while the Israelites wandered in the desert.

Notice how Moses was prepared to lead the Israelites out of Egypt and manage two million people (approximately) while travelling for forty years in the desert (a herculean task in itself). If you think about it, there probably were not many people, if any, able to lead the exodus. God prepared a very needed leader, starting many years before that need! Look at the miracles of Moses's preparation to lead the Exodus: not being killed when Pharaoh ordered all newborn Israelite boys to be killed, floating in a basket on the Nile, found by Pharaoh's daughter, and his mother becoming Moses's nursemaid, wet nurse!

Growing up in Pharaoh's household with the highest quality of training and education he could possibly receive, at that time in the world, there was probably no more sophisticated training to become a leader than in that very place. Then when Moses was a young man, God had some other additional training for him. Moses ended up in the wilderness by himself as a shepherd, exposed to loneliness and coming to the awareness of life and nature when there was that much time to think, then rounding out his development by becoming a husband and father.

Then it became time, in God's plan, for God's people to be freed from slavery and travel home to their Promised Land.

I have always wondered, why didn't God change Pharaoh's heart, and He would then let God's people leave? We know God has that power, why did He not use it? Why did God keep hardening Pharaoh's heart (which added more and more punishment to the Egyptian people)?

We do not know all God's reasons, but Scripture makes one very clear. God demanded that He be recognized as the one and only God and be glorified by the Egyptians.

> Then the Lord said to Moses, "Go to Pharaoh for I have hardened his heart and the hearts of his courtiers in order that I may display these (plagues), my signs among them." (**Exodus 10:1**)

> I displayed my signs among them in order that you **may know I am the Lord**. (**Exodus 10:2**)

> Lord stiffened Pharaoh's heart. (**Exodus 10:20**)

> ...stiffen Pharaoh's heart, and he will pursue to the Red Sea. (**Exodus 14:4**)

> ...that **I might gain glory** through Pharaoh and all his host, and the Egyptians **shall know I am Lord**. (**Exodus 7:5** and **14:8**)

Lord stiffened the heart of Pharaoh. (**Exodus 9:12**)

...miracles had been performed (before Pharaoh), but the Lord had stiffened the heart of Pharaoh. (**Exodus 11:10**)

...will harden Pharaoh's heart that I might multiply my signs and marvels in the land of Egypt. (**Exodus 7:3**)

Do you get the feeling that God was a little upset that the Egyptians thought Pharaoh was a god, and they also worshiped their other gods and, in addition, had mistreated God's people and kept them in slavery?

Let us review God's ETERNAL PLAN here:

- He promised that the Israelites were His chosen people, and they would someday enter the Promised Land of their future, Canaan.
- In their journey to the Promised Land, God caused them to be brought to Egypt by all the hardships in Joseph's journey. They then remained there for 430 years, part as favored guests and then enslaved later. For what purpose, we do not know! Question: What amount of faith, patience, and persistence did it take by the Israelites all those years?
- But when it was time to be freed and leave Egypt, God sent His messengers, Moses and Aaron, and performed many miracles to prove the God of the Israelites was the one and only God and was real and more powerful than any other gods and was to be glorified.

Note: The miracles continued to protect God's chosen people because the Israelites (approximately two million people) were freed and entered the wilderness where they were completely dependent on God for food and water every day for their forty-year journey before they entered their Promised Homeland. I hope you are impressed with the magnitude of the exodus journey and the miracles required for that journey to be successful, and it was successful!

I hope your heart and mind are touched by these two examples of the glorification of God and the extreme good that comes out of extreme suffering on the part of God's children. I think they are wonderful testimonies to the fact that God has an Eternal Plan for the earth and for each of His children on the earth, and in His timing and His manner, He will fulfill His plan.

It is obvious that your situation is not of the magnitude of these stories, but the principle is still the same for you. What happened to you had meaning because it was part of God's Eternal Plan for you, so the confusion, fear, and hurt you are suffering is for something that had purpose and meaning. Your healing will result in the purposes God has for you in your new life.

OUR NEED FOR A SAVIOR—WAS THERE A PLAN?

Did God have an Eternal Plan for you and me when man could not live by God's laws given on Mount Sinai and later on? Enter Jesus, our Savior. All the happenings in Jesus's life matched completely as prophesized in the Old Testament and by Jesus in the New Testament **(Luke 9:22, 18:32–33, 24:44–47, and 24:25–26). God had an Eternal Plan to provide us a savior because He knew we would need one!**

WHAT DOES GOD SAY ABOUT HAVING AN ETERNAL PLAN AND PURPOSE?

> So shall my Word be that comes from my mouth; it shall not return to me empty, but it shall **accomplish that which I purpose**, and

shall succeed in the thing for which I sent it. **(Isaiah 55:11)**

The Lord will fulfill **His purpose for m**e; your steadfast love, O Lord, endures forever. **(Psalm 138:8)**

The Lord has **made everything for its purpose. (Proverbs 16:4)**

My counsel shall stand, and I shall stand, **and I will accomplish all my purpose. (Isaiah 46:10)**

I have spoken, and I will bring it to pass; **I have purposed, and I will do it. (Isaiah 46:11)**

I know that you can do all things, and that no **purpose of yours can be thwarted. (Job 42:2)**

Blessed be the God and Father of our Lord Jesus Christ who has blessed us in Christ with every **spiritual blessing in the heavenly places** even as **He chose us in Him before the foundation of the world** that we should be holy and blameless before Him. In love, he **predestined** us for adoption to Himself as sons through Jesus Christ, **according to the purpose of His will**, to the praise of His glorious grace, with which he has blessed us in the beloved. In Him, we have redemption through His blood, the forgiveness of our trespasses, according to the riches of His grace, which He lavished upon us in all wisdom and insight, **making known to us the mystery of**

His will according to his purpose, which He set forth in Christ as a plan for the fullness of time, to unite all things in Him, things in Heaven and things on earth.

In him, we have obtained an inheritance, having been predestined **according to the purpose of Him who works all things according to the counsel of His will** so that we who were the first to hope in Christ might be to the praise of His glory. In him, you also, when you heard the Word of Truth, the gospel of your salvation, and believed in Him, were sealed with the promised Holy Spirit who is the guarantee of our inheritance until we acquire possession of it to the praise of His glory. (**Ephesians 1:3–14**)

But as it is written, what no eye has seen, nor ear heard, nor the heart of man imagined, **what God has prepared for those who love Him.** (**1 Corinthians 2:9**)

According to the **eternal purpose that He has realized in** Christ Jesus, our Lord, in whom we have boldness and access with confidence through our faith in Him. (**Ephesians 3:11–12**)

Men of Israel, hear these words: Jesus of Nazareth, a man attested to you by God with mighty works and wonders and signs that God did through Him in your midst, as you yourselves know—this Jesus delivered up **according to the definite plan and foreknowledge of God.** (Acts 2:22–23)

He made from one man every nation of mankind to live on all the face of the earth, having determined allotted periods and the boundaries of their dwelling place that they should seek God and perhaps feel their way toward Him and find Him, yet He is actually not far from each one of us. (**Acts 17:26–28**)

For it is **God who works in you, both to will and to work for His good pleasure**. (**Philippians 2:13**)

The counsel of the Lord stands forever **the plans of His heart** to all generations. (**Psalm 33:11**)

WHAT IS GOD'S ETERNAL PLAN? THE BIBLE TELLS US THE BEGINNING AND END OF GOD'S ETERNAL PLAN.

- God created the Heavens and the earth.
- He placed perfect human beings (Adam and Eve) in a perfect place (Garden of Eden) for perfect fellowship with God.
- Then sin ruined that perfect relationship.
- Then God provided the Ten Commandments and the law to recapture the perfect relationship with Him, but man could not follow the law.
- Then in place of the law, God sacrificed Jesus for future forgiveness of sin.
- And now He waits for all man to hear His gospel message, and when He is ready, Jesus will come a second time to take His children to Heaven and have that desired perfect relationship with God in Heaven for eternity.

What does the Bible say about how my situation fits into God's Eternal Plan?

How does that help me cope with my situation now?

- God's **ETERNAL PLAN** gives us a **TODAY** and a **TOMORROW** because He created us to be in fellowship with Him today and for eternity.
- He gives us hope **TODAY** because of the following:
  - Each one's personal relationship with God
  - His love for each one of us
  - His promises to protect and strengthen us
  - His promises to encourage us and provide for us
- The Holy Spirit, being within us to discern truth and, thus, have wisdom
- We have an opportunity to serve God's children.
- We have an opportunity to glorify God.
- His promises that everything that happens is to glorify Him and/or for good, for those who love Him

  And we know that for those who love God, all things work together for good for those who are called according to His purpose. (**Romans 8:28**)

- He gives us His **FUTURE** (Heaven) which gives us **HOPE** for **TOMORROW**.

  Jesus has removed the "sting of death" and replaced it with eternal life. Resurrection from the dead or taken up to Heaven if alive, and our mortal body will become immortal, immortality and a dwelling place in the house of the Lord forever (Heaven). (**1 Corinthians 15:50–57**)

...according to His great mercy, He has caused us to be born again to a **living hope** through the resurrection of Jesus Christ from the dead, to an inheritance that is imperishable, undefiled, and unfading kept in Heaven for you. (**1 Peter 1:3–4**)

...we ourselves, who have the first fruits of the Spirit, groan inwardly as we wait eagerly for our adoption as sons, the redemption of our bodies. For in this hope, we were saved. Now hope that is seen is not hope. For who hopes for what he sees? But if **we hope for what we do not see, we wait for it with patience.** (**Romans 8:23–25**)

WHAT IS GOD'S PLAN FOR ME? WHY AM I STILL HERE?

Yes, He has a total **Eternal Plan**, and what has happened to your life is a part of it. You are part of it. You are loved, known, and have a role to play in God's plan for you.

But as it is written, eye has not seen, nor ear heard, neither have entered into the heart of man, the **things which God hath prepared for them that love Him**. (**1 Corinthians 2:9–10**)

...**for it is God who works in you, both to will and to work for His good pleasure.** (**Philippians 2:12**)

So shall my word be that goes from my mouth; it shall not return to me empty, but it **shall accomplish that which I purpose** and

149

shall succeed in the thing for which I sent it. (**Isaiah 55:11**)

Men of Israel, hear these words: Jesus of Nazareth, a man attested to you by God with mighty works and wonders and signs that God did through Him in your midst, as you yourselves know this Jesus, **delivered up according to the definite plan and fore-knowledge of God**. (Acts 2:22–23)

And I am sure of this that he who began a good work in you will bring it to completion at the day of Jesus Christ. (**Philippians 1:6**)

The counsel of the Lord stands forever, **the plans of His heart** to all generations. (**Psalm 33:11**)

The natural question is "what is God's plan for me? What am I supposed to do now?" I need answers right away!

I wish I, or anyone else, could give you answers. But right now, the best thing you can do is to retain and keep improving your relationship with God. I believe He will lead you and provide direction for your purpose in your **NEW LIFE**. God will direct and provide if you are looking, listening, and praying. I know Scripture and programs are not clear sometimes on what you should be doing in your life; but God will provide. Keep searching, **be patient**, little steps at a time!

I believe that if you have a thankful mental attitude, you will be surprised at what you see that God puts right in front of you to do.

Do not make the mistake of thinking you will not be happy unless you are working on some big important purpose. With a servant's attitude, nothing is too small if it is in God's purpose.

PRACTICAL STEPS TOWARD HEALING— SMART

What do I have to do to dig my way out of this pit of loneliness, confusion, fear, and hurt?

Do I just keep "Goin' and Doin'" whatever I face in life until time has dulled down my emotions and softened my hurt? Do I just settle for a bearable/livable life?

Is there any better choice?

Yes! To heal and have a meaningful and fulfilled new future life, you need to get **SMART** and act **SMART**.

SMART is an acronym for

S—serve others

M—mental—Embrace an "attitude of gratitude" daily.

A—activities—Participate in activities that have a loving and caring environment.

R—relationships with people

T—time—It will take time! Be nice to yourself and give yourself time!

Before we discuss these areas you must concentrate on to heal, let me call to your attention the reason these areas are the most important for your healing. They work!

Notice that four of the five areas involve **people** who are being inserted into, or retained, in your new life activities while healing. Remember, **grief tends to isolate a survivor, but love and SMART** will bring a survivor back into the circle of a meaningful and fulfilled life.

Why are people so important to a survivor's healing? Think about your life before your loss. Were people a big or small part of your life? I believe people, whether closely or distantly related, being in your life were the main determinant of whether you enjoyed life or not. **People acknowledge your existence, react to you, care about you, help you and many other inter-relationships that affirm you as a person.** What would life be without people?

No matter how bad you feel, how much confusion, fear, and hurt you feel right now, you must know that working toward **relating with people** is a **major part of healing**.

I recognize that acting "SMART" will be difficult, and healing will not happen right away. **Just take little steps at a time!** Little victories will happen. Remember, everyone is different, and each one starts from a different place in their healing.

I know how paralyzing and disabling your grief can be at the start. I am tempted to write that you should start the healing steps of **SMART** when you are emotionally ready. But **no matter what emotional state you are in, and no matter how you feel, you should start participating in these SMART areas as much as you can and as soon as possible.**

It is little steps at a time, large results are not going to happen right away. The hardest part of your journey of healing are those first steps. Get up, get dressed, and get out of the house!

(S)MART = Serving others is healing.

One of the best things you can do for yourself is to serve others. Why? Because that is all **it takes for you to be out of yourself** and your confusion, fear, and hurt, and it makes you focus on someone else and their needs, at least for a period of time. In fact, sometimes you will find that, although your situation is hurtful, the person being helped is in even worse shape.

How do you feel when you have served someone and helped them? The results I have seen are that it is very therapeutic in many ways: **You achieve a sense of accomplishment**, being **valuable to someone, doing a good, helpful thing**, a very **all-round positive experience at a time** when you need it. It gives you **worth and significance**.

Recognize the **therapeutic aspects of serving**:

- You did something that was needed, and you were needed.
- You gave your time, talent, and energy sacrificially, proving you are a **loving, caring person**.
- Your self-image and confidence are enhanced because you have a **greater purpose and broader perspective on other people's need**s.
- There is a good chance you **created a new relationship or reinforced an existing relationship** with someone who may become more of a part of your new life, **a new friend or a greater friend when you need them the most!**
- One of the major parts of God's personal plan for you is that He wants you to love and serve other people. So serving others in any small way will help to start making your life more meaningful and fulfilled right now!

The reason serving others works is because **Scripture tells us that a main part of our life's purpose is to serve God and His children.**

But whoever would be great among you **must be your servant**, and whoever would be first among you must be your slave—even as the **Son of man came not to be served but to serve** and to give His life as a ransom for many. **(Matthew 20:26–28)**

For you were called to freedom, brothers. Only, do not use your freedom as an opportunity for the flesh **but through love, serve one another. For the whole law is fulfilled in one word; you shall love your neighbor as yourself.** **(Galatians 5:13)**

So if there is any encouragement in Christ, any comfort from love, any participation in the spirit, any affection and sympathy, complete my joy by being of the same mind, having the same love, being in full accord and of one mind. **Do nothing from selfish ambition or conceit, but in humility, count others more significant that yourselves.** Let each of you look not only to his self-interests but also to the interest of others. Have this mind among yourselves, which is yours in Christ Jesus... **(He) emptied Himself by taking the form of a servant. (Philippians 2:1–4)**

Above all, keep loving one another earnestly since love covers a multitude of sins. Show hospitality to one another without grumbling. As each has received a gift, use it to serve one another as good stewards of God's varied grace... Whoever **serves by the strength that God supplies in order that in**

everything God may be glorified through Jesus Christ. (1 Peter 4:8–11)

By this, we know what love is: That He laid down his life for us, and we ought to lay down our lives for our brothers. **(1 John 3–16)**

If you pour yourself out for the hungry and satisfy the desire of the afflicted, then shall your light rise in the darkness and your gloom be as the noonday. (Isaiah 58:10)

For though I am free from all, I have made myself a servant to all... (1 Corinthians 9:19)

Let us not love in word or talk but in deed and truth. (1 John 3:18)

Think about your circle of relationships. It starts at the home and advances to family. Do not forget your neighbors, work associates, church members, and friends. Get started, and you will be blessed with healing.

S(M)ART = MENTAL ATTITUDE
DEVELOP AND PRACTICE HAVING AN "ATTITUDE OF GRATITUDE."

Read this section of **SMART** very closely! Understanding and practicing the proper **mental attitude from now on will be the major factor in your healing.**

The more positive, full of hope, and anticipation your mental attitude becomes, the quicker and more effective your healing begins.

Survivors who have acquired the proper mental attitude heal to the point where they **end up with a meaningful, fulfilled life instead of only a bearable/livable life.**

I am sure you have heard somewhere along the way that your brain is one of the most sophisticated computers in the world. It has unlimited abilities. **Your mind** is so **powerful that it dominates and controls all aspects of your life.**

King Solomon, the oldest and wisest man in Israel, knew the power of thinking.

> As a man thinketh in his heart, so is he.
> (**Proverbs 23:7 KJV**)

And old Dr. Seuss had it right:

> My thoughts determine who I am. (**Dr. Seuss**)

Why is our mental attitude so important?

> Thoughts lead on to purpose, purpose leads on to actions, actions form habits, habits decide character which fixes our destiny. (**Tryon Edwards**)

> A man is a product of his thoughts. What he thinks he becomes. (**Mahatma Gandhi**)

> The world we have created is a product of our thinking, it cannot be changed without changing our thinking. (**Albert Einstein**)

Consequently, if your mind is not right, nothing else will be.

What one allows to go into their mind, which they harbor there, is extremely important. The better thoughts in, the better results out (i.e., healing and a meaningful and fulfilled new life).

Something that you must understand about developing your mental attitude is that circumstances are going to happen to you. Some are good, some bad. **But what really matters is how you react to them!**

> It is not the events that shape my life that determine how I feel and act, but rather, it's the way I interpret and evaluate my life experiences. (**Tony Robbins**)

You have a choice. You can let bad things (trials and tribulations) cause you to take on a mental attitude of unfairness and defeat and slowly slip down into depression and despair, or you can react in a trusting, hopeful, and positive way.

So no matter how bad something is that happens to you, it can only lead you into long-term heartbreak and defeat if you let it. It is how you react to it that counts.

> There is nothing good or bad, but thinking makes it so. (**William Shakespeare**)

We are charged with **renewing our mind, so we react properly, in God's eyes, to what life throws at us.**

> Put off your old self, **be renewed in the spirit of your minds, and to put on the new self, created after the likeness of God** in true righteousness and holiness. (**Ephesians 4:22–24**)

> ...take every thought captive to obey Christ. (**2 Corinthians 10:5**)

> Do not be conformed to this world, but be transformed by the renewal of your mind. (**Romans 12:2**)

> And have put on the **new self**, which is being
> renewed in knowledge after the image of its
> creator. (**Colossians 3:10**)

A very effective way to start is to truly develop a thankful spirit based upon your present life. Stop and think. Write down those things one so easily takes for granted. Make a list. Keep adding to it.

I would imagine right now you are saying, "Wait a minute, amid all my confusion, fear, and hurt, you want me to think positive and start being thankful? I understand the value of being positive, and I would like to be, but what do I have to be positive about right now?"

Agreed! There is no doubt that a survivor's initial mental attitude goes spinning down deep into the negative and hurtful thoughts of confusion, fear, hurt, and despair.

Admittedly, it is not reasonable to ask a survivor to put on a smile and think and act positively right away. **But remember that a long race begins with one step. Start today!**

Cultivating and exercising a thankful spirit is a good beginning to get you thinking to a positive level it needs to reach to heal.

THANKFULNESS turns into APPRECIATION, which turns into ACCEPTANCE, which becomes SATISFACTION AND A PEACEFUL COUNTENANCE.

If we can just get past that invisible blanket of grief and its effects on us, **there seems to be many reasons to be thankful:**

- You, the survivor, are still here! You have a life to live, **a life that God still has a purpose for!**
- You have God's Word to instruct you, to live by, and to enjoy the results. You are never alone.
- You can rely on all the promises of God that gives you worthiness, importance, safety, and the enjoyment of life.

+ You are surrounded by what God has provided for you in your daily living (i.e., people, sustenance, environment, job, etc.), anything and everything that most miss in their hurried lives. Miracles are all around you every day that can be missed. All one must do is to look and appreciate God's miracles of life around us!

YOU CAN BE THANKFUL BECAUSE THERE IS HOPE FOR THE FUTURE.

But we do not want you to be uninformed, brothers, about those who are asleep **that you may not grieve as others do who have no hope**. For since we believe that Jesus died and rose again, even so, through Jesus, God will bring with Him those who have fallen asleep. (**1 Thessalonians 4:13–14**)

Blessed is the man who remains steadfast under trial, for when he has stood the test, he will receive the crown of life that God has promised to those who love Him. (**James 1:12**)

Therefore, since we have been justified by faith, we have peace with God through our Lord Jesus Christ. Through Him, we have also obtained access by faith into this grace in which we stand, and we rejoice in **HOPE** of the **glory of God**. Not only that, but **we rejoice in our sufferings, knowing that suffering produces endurance, and endurance produces character, and character produced hope. And hope does not put us to shame because God's love has been poured into**

our hearts through the Holy Spirit, who he has been given to us. (Romans 5:1–5)

You can be thankful because of the trust and faith you can have in a good God and good results.

Blessed is the man who **remains steadfast under trial,** because when he has stood the test, **he will receive the crown of life that God has promised** to those who love Him. **(James 1:12)**

...who comforts us in all our affliction so that we may be able to comfort those who are **in any affliction** with the comfort with which we ourselves are comforted by God. For **as we share abundantly in Christ's sufferings, so through Christ, we share abundantly in comfort too. (2 Corinthians 1:4–5)**

Scripture That Reinforces Having a Thankful Spirit

Rejoice always, pray without ceasing, give thanks in all circumstances; for this is the will of God in Christ Jesus for you. (1 Thessalonians 5:16:18)

A joyful heart is good medicine, but a crushed spirit dries up the bones. (**Proverbs 17:22**)

For **I have learned in whatever situation I am to be content**. I know how to be brought low, and I know how to abound. In any and every circumstance, **I have learned the secret of facing plenty and hunger, abundance,**

and need. I can do all things through Him who strengthens me. (Philippians 4:11–14)

Be content with what you have for He has said, "I will never leave you nor forsake you." **(Hebrews 13:5)**

Rejoice in the Lord always; again I will say, rejoice. Let your reasonableness be known to everyone. The Lord is at hand; do not be anxious about anything, but **in everything, by prayer and supplication with thanksgiving, let your requests be made known to God.** And the peace of God, which surpasses all understanding, **will guard your hearts and your minds in Christ Jesus. Finally, brothers, whatever is true, whatever is honorable, whatever is just, whatever is pure, whatever is lovely, whatever is commendable, if there is any excellence, if there is anything worthy of praise, think about these things. (Philippians 4:4–8)**

Set your mind on things that are above, not on things that are on the earth. (Colossians 3:2)

...and be thankful. Let the Word of Christ dwell in you richly with thankfulness in your hearts to God. (Colossians 3:15–16)

When the righteous cry for help, the Lord hears them and delivers them out of all their troubles. **The Lord is near to the brokenhearted and saves the crushed in spirit. (Psalm 34:17–18)**

> For **He delivers the needy when he calls the poor and Him who has no helper**. (**Psalm 72:12**)

Your mind is one of the **most powerful computers in the world**. Using computer language, remember, **"if junk goes in, expect junk to come out!"**

Do not waste this wonderful gift God gave to you. We want to work toward eliminating negative thinking. And negative results.

We are working toward "recognition of blessings, thankfulness, and appreciation going in and feeling loved, protected, enabled, and worthy coming out."

God's Word tells us to dwell in God's Word and keep seeking Him. God wants us to keep putting His Word into our minds and heart.

> **Blessed is the man...his delight is in the law of the Lord, and on His law, He mediates day and night.** (**Psalm 1:1–2**)

> **The law of the Lord is perfect, reviving** the soul; the testimony of the Lord is sure, **making wise** the simple; the precepts of the Lord are right, **rejoicing the heart**; the commandment of the Lord is pure, **enlightening the eyes**; the fear of the Lord is clean, enduring forever; the rules of the Lord are true and righteous altogether. More to be desired are they than gold, even much fine gold, sweeter also than honey and drippings of the honeycomb. Moreover, by them is your servant warned; **in keeping them, there is great reward.** (**Psalm 19:7–11**)

You **keep him in perfect peace whose mind is stayed on you**, because He trusts in you. **(Isaiah 26:3)**

What better input could there be? Precious treasures in; precious results out!

From *The Power of Your Attitude* by Stan Toler

Your **THOUGHTS** shape your **IDENTITY**
As a man thinketh in his heart, so is he. **(Proverbs 23:7 KJV)**
Your **WORDS** become your **REALITY**
Your **ACTIONS** determine your **CHARACTER**
Your **HABITS** predict your **FUTURE**
Your **CHOICES** change your **LIFE!** Choose:
HOPE
HUMILITY
GRATITUDE
GENEROSITY
COMPASSION
JOY
PERSEVERANCE

SM(A)RT = ACTIVITIES

I know your emotions may be all over the place, and you do not have much energy; but activities are very important. They **get you moving**, and very importantly, they **involve contact with people**.

Preferred activities would be with others **in a loving and caring atmosphere**, such as with survivors who have lost loved ones. Also, grief-oriented classes or meetings of any kind will help you heal.

The biggest benefit of doing so (even though you don't feel like it right now) is because **you can plan to be with "wounded warriors" who can empathize with you and will care about** you. LOVE **heals all in the long run, and you need love and support from the very beginning.**

You may not feel like you get much from these activities at first, but your subconscious mind has heard much, and it will be recalled when you are ready.

"When you are ready for the next step" in your healing process, it is going to be up to you. **You are going to heal much quicker if you keep being SMART and doing SMART.** As an example, I have had survivor participants in my Grieving with Hope program come back again as many as four times. What they said after each time was that it was **immensely helpful because "they heard things they did not hear"** the other **times**. Doesn't that make sense? A survivor is on an emotional roller coaster and very understandably might not be ready to hear or want to hear something they need to hear at that time. Hey! I did not take it personally that they did not hear everything I presented over an eight-week program! It just makes common sense. Just keep moving and learning and sharing love in activities wherever you can.

Participants in my Grieving with Hope programs have come one week, up to ten years, after they have lost a loved one. Since they are uniquely different, each hears and are touched by something different, but **they do hear and eventually heal!**

Activities you need to START doing:

- **Learn about and deal with the difficult things of grief.**
- **Get up, shower/bathe, eat, read your Bible.**
- **Connect with God every day—pray, pray, pray.**
- **Journal your feelings and experiences.**
- **Get out of the house.**
- **Build new patterns and interests.**
- **Find opportunities for Christian fellowship—Bible studies, etc.**

Some caveats:

- **Be careful of becoming too busy.**
- **Avoid unhealthy relationships.**

Activities you **need to STOP doing:**

- **Getting isolated from people**
- **Not being nice to yourself**
- **Not eating right**
- **Not showering/bathing**
- **Not exercising**

Any activities with Christian brothers and sisters expose you to lovers of God and **lovers of you.** Church services, Bible studies, and other activities provided by the church are all recommended as the most beneficial.

Any positive activity where you get out of the house will most likely be helpful.

I know you do not feel like it sometimes, but get up, get dressed, get out among people, and experience the healing influence of relating with people, whether directly or indirectly. My only requirement is that there be a loving and caring atmosphere wherever you go.

SMA(R)T = RELATIONSHIPS

Now, more than ever, you need to deepen any relationship you have had with anyone in the past or any **new relationships** you have because of your **SMART** activities.

Why this sudden need to deepen relationships? Remember, **grief tends to isolate you** (i.e., **loss of support** of many after a few months, people not knowing what to say to you or do for you, no energy, no care, confusion, etc.). **You are virtually being isolated. Your well-being, your recovery, and healing are entirely on YOU.**

You need to find one person, if you are lucky, but even more than one, if possible, true friends who you can trust and will be loyal to you **to a point of sacrificial love with their time and energy.**

There is one true friend you can have for sure—that is the value of having faith in God, His love, and His promises for you. He has promised that He will always be there and never forsake you. What an anchor in your troubled time!

But you still need a close friend or friends that will **help you get through the emotional stages and periods of doubt and disappointment that you are going to experience.**

I want you to conduct your **SM(Activities)RT** in a **loving and caring atmosphere** for the support that it will provide you. Just as important, get to work on deepening your **relationship** with the one person or more you are going to really rely on. This may be a fearful, but necessary, step in healing.

Someone in your family is the most likely, but you will recognize who really cares about you and your happiness. Who has God put in your life? Ask Him. Step back. Look and see.

Do not hold back with the one you have chosen, ask for their help (including time and energy), tell them your true feelings (do not hold back), set up some planned meeting times and activities with them, ask them to go with you to your activities, etc.

If you do not have time to talk or ask enough for some reason, **write out your needs and state of mind** and send them to your trusted friend/s, little steps but forming a deeper, deeper, deeper relationship.

Remember, some people who knew your loved one **may also be suffering from grief themselves and may not be able to help you with the relationship needs you have at this time**. In fact, they may need help and understanding, themselves, from a wounded warrior like you when you are able. They are probably not the person to choose.

Deepening your relationship with God and a support person/s is the most important thing you can do. They are invaluable to your healing!

Feel your feelings, and express them verbally or in writing as much as possible.

> Bear one another's burdens, and so fulfill the
> law of Christ. (**Galatians 6:2**)

SMAR(T) = TIME—GIVE YOURSELF TIME TO HEAL PROPERLY.

Time, wonderful time, alleviates some or all the pressure on a survivor. It allows each unique survivor to **heal in their own unique way and in their own time** (necessities and emergencies being the exception).

A survivor's healing is not on the clock, and no one should put that pressure on someone who is hurting.

Most importantly, be nice to yourself! Do not compare yourself to others. Eliminate any "should haves," "have tos," "could haves," and other demanding phrases, past, present, or future.

Question: How could anyone else have any valid idea how long it should take unique you to heal?

Give yourself TIME to adjust and live up to your expectations. Remember that there is no typical response to the loss of a loved one because **there is no typical loss of a loved one. EVERYONE IS DIFFERENT!**

When my wife died, I did not do all of these valuable things contained in SMART I am suggesting for you to do; but I wish I had talked or written more to my family and trusted friends and kept them posted about where I was emotionally and needs. How I regret that. But I did not know it would be the right thing to do then. But now you know. Write or talk about how you feel and where you are without hesitation.

CHAPTER 22

HOW DOES THE BIBLE TELL ME TO THINK AND ACT AS A CHRISTIAN IN GOOD TIMES AND BAD?

Oh! How I love the Scripture's instructions! I know that they are right, and they work! We, in our humanness, just must strive to be more like Jesus and live these principles!

Living these directions make the good times even better as we are more appreciative of our situation, and they help us work our way through the bad times, thus, reducing the amount of confusion, fear, and hurt we experience.

Strive for Christian maturity, which is to take on the character of Jesus.

> May grace and peace be multiplied to you **in the knowledge of God and of Jesus, our Lord.**
>
> His divine power has **granted to us all things that pertain to life and godliness** through the knowledge of Him who called

us to his own glory and excellence **by which He has granted to us His precious and very great promises** so that through them, you **may become partakers of the divine nature,** having escaped from the corruption that is in the world because of sinful desire. For this very reason, **make every effort to supplement your faith** with virtue, and virtue with **knowledge,** and knowledge with **self-control,** and self-control with steadfastness, and **steadfastness** with godliness, and godliness with brotherly affection, and **brotherly affection with love.** For if these qualities are yours and increasing, they keep you from being ineffective or unfruitful in the knowledge of our Lord, Jesus Christ. For whoever lacks these qualities is so nearsighted that he is blind, having forgotten that he was cleansed from his former sins. Therefore, brothers, be even more diligent to confirm your calling and election, for **if you practice these qualities, you will never** fail. For in this way, there will be richly **provided for you an entrance into the eternal kingdom** of our Lord and Savior Jesus Christ. (**2 Peter 1:2–11**)

Rejoice in the Lord always; again I will say, rejoice. Let your reasonableness be known to everyone. The Lord is at hand; **do not be anxious about anything,** but **in everything by prayer and supplication with thanksgiving,** let your requests be made known to God. **And the peace of God, which surpasses all understanding,** will guard your hearts and your minds in Christ Jesus. (**Philippians 4:5–7**)

Finally, brothers, whatever is true, whatever is honorable, whatever is just, whatever is pure, whatever is lovely, whatever is commendable, if there is any excellence, if there is anything worthy of praise, think about these things. What you have earned and received and heard and seen in me—practice these things, and the God of peace will be with you. **(Philippians 4:8)**

He (God) has told you, O man, what is good; and what does the Lord require of you but to **do justice, and to love kindness, and to walk humbly with your God? (Micah 6:8)**

How am I to act in the bad times and the good?

I know how to be brought low, and I know how to abound. In any and every circumstance, I have learned the secret of facing plenty and hunger, abundance, and need. **I can do all things through him who strengthens me. (Philippians 4:12–13)**

Rejoice always, pray without ceasing, give thanks in all circumstances; for this is the will of God in Christ Jesus for you. **(1 Thessalonians 5:16)**

James, a servant of God and of the Lord, Jesus Christ, to the twelve tribes in the Dispersion: Greetings.
　　Count it all joy, my brothers, when you meet trials of various kinds, for you know that the **testing of your faith produces steadfastness**. And let steadfastness have its

full effect **that you may be perfect and complete, lacking in nothing**.

If any of you lacks wisdom, let him ask God who gives generously to all without reproach, and it will be given him. But let him ask in faith, with no doubting, for the one who doubts is like a wave of the sea that is driven and tossed by the wind. For that person must not suppose that he will receive anything from the Lord; he is a double-minded man, unstable in all his ways.

Let the lowly brother boast in his exaltation, and the rich in his humiliation, because like a flower of the grass, he will pass away. For the sun rises with its scorching heat and withers the grass; its flower falls, and its beauty perishes. So also will the rich man fade away in the midst of his pursuits.

Blessed is the man who remains steadfast under trial, for when he has stood the test, he will receive the crown of life, which God has promised to those who love Him. (James 1:1–12)

I have set the Lord always before me; because He is at my right hand, I shall not be shaken. Therefore, my heart is glad and my whole being rejoices. My flesh also dwells secure. You make known to me the path of life, in your presence there is fullness of joy; at your right hand are pleasures forevermore. (Psalm 16:8–11)

I am sure you can see that these biblical directions fit right in with the SMART recovery plan (i.e., in having a mental attitude of thankfulness and a positive attitude).

Hang in there! It is so hard! Apply these characteristics in your life as much as possible—little steps, little victories, and then big victories and healing to a meaningful and purposeful life.

CHAPTER 23

HOW TO SUPPORT
AND BE SUPPORTED

How your support people can help you—it's all about you, not them!
How you can help support other survivors—it's all about them, not you!

Help From Your Support People

What can others do to help support you?

I have been told by survivors the following attempts to be helpful have been said to them:

- It has been a while since you lost your loved one. Isn't it about time you are healing and moving on?
- I am sure your loss hurts, and a lot of different emotions have arisen. But shouldn't you have gotten control of your emotions by now and not be so emotional about things?
- I am worried about you. I know some survivors that have moved on in their life. They have cleaned out a lot

of closets and gotten rid of things that you have kept. Surely those things must keep reminding you of your loss. Is keeping those things helpful?

- Is it healthy for you to keep continuing traditions and remembering memories?
- Different comments made like "you should" or "should not" be doing things. Why didn't you do something about...? Maybe it is better if you...? I would think you would be changing (in some specific way). Shouldn't you be doing better by now?

Argh! How about the following common comments that people who are trying to help say and what you would like to say back to them:

Comment: I know how you feel.
Response: Unless you have experienced the loss of a loved one, you have no idea how much confusion, fear, and hurt I feel!
Comment: It is God's will.
Response: I am too upset to have you explain that to me right now and, seriously, are you able to explain what you just said?
Comment: God promised He would not give you more that you can handle.
Response: Right now in my emotional state, it seems that maybe God has forgotten He made that promise to me.

A support person must understand that because of the **uniqueness** of the survivor, most of the support person's opinions on what the survivor should do are not helpful. Unfortunately, the support person's personal life experiences are not the survivor's unique life experiences. Consequently, in trying to give support, it is more important to **listen, listen, listen**, then the listener inserting their thoughts and try to solve all the problems and get the survivor healed as soon as possible.

That means talk very little and use talk that only searches further into the survivor's condition or state of mind, and let them tell you! It should be all about the survivor and what physical and mental condition they are in and what is needed to help them. It is not about the support person and what they think needs to be done by the survivor.

The goal is to find out where the survivor is in their physical and mental condition and accept them where they are and start from there. **The survivor wants to be heard (listened to) and authenticated (accepted where they are) more than anything.** Knowing this is especially important for the support person, because if they judge the survivor by the support person's standards, the survivor's timing and healing needs are not coordinating with what the support person expects to happen. In that situation, the support person can become discouraged or get in a hurry for healing, and their support may wane or disappear.

Losing the support of those family and friends, who really wanted to help you, is a very sad and disappointing result. This can be a major setback in a survivor's healing because those people you really were going to depend on are not there when you need them the most.

How can the remaining support people who you are depending on the most disappear or fall off in their support? **Can't they see how much you are hurting and so confused and need help?**

I think that another reason that people you depend on for support are not as helpful as you expected (and note, the reason you are not as helpful as you want to be with other survivors who need your support) is that the support person does not know what to say or do. Your support people, and you, were not prepared to deal with the loss of a loved one or help someone who has lost a loved one. The usual reason that support people hold back and "don't say or do" is because they do not know what to say or what to do and are afraid if they "say or do," they will hurt the feelings of the survivor. The elephant is in the room, but the survivor does not get much help because everybody, including the survivor, is afraid they might hurt someone else's feelings if they bring up the subject of the loved one's death. Good intentions all around but not helpful to the one who lost their loved one. That is why "feeling your feelings" and "expressing them properly" is so important.

LISTEN, LISTEN, LISTEN! Be there for and with the survivor as long as it is necessary. Just being there alongside is extremely important—no goals, no time criteria, no feelings criteria, no back to normal criteria, just caring.

Listen to and be with the survivor and let them heal in their own unique way and timing. If you cannot do that, then you are not going to be of help. **It is all about the survivor not about the support person.** Think about this:

> When we honestly ask ourselves which person in our lives means the most, we often find that it is those who—instead of giving much advice, solutions, or cures—have chosen rather to share our pain and touch our wounds with a gentle and tender hand. The friend who can be silent with us in a moment of despair or confusion, who can stay with us in an hour of grief and bereavement, who can tolerate not knowing, not curing, not healing and face with us the reality of our powerlessness, that is a friend who cares. (**Henri Nouwen**)

In the Bible, Job's friends did the right thing at first. During the time of heartaches and sicknesses that Job experienced, they gathered around him. They were with him but said nothing. But after seven days, apparently, they could not stand it anymore and started trying to solve his problems. They started talking and asking questions as to who did something wrong to cause Job's situation. Then Job said, "A fine bunch of friends you are."

They were not being helpful. They were judging Job by their own philosophies and standards rather than listening and being there for Job. As the story turns out, Job's hardship was not caused by him or anyone else doing something wrong. They were caused by the devil testing Job's faithfulness to his God.

Job ultimately went from complete tragedy to triumph when God replaced his family and all his material losses with two times what he had lost.

LISTEN, LISTEN, LISTEN AND JUST BE THERE FOR A SURVIVOR THAT ONE IS TRYING TO HELP. If you cannot do that, then you are not going to be of help.

Remember, as much as others try to help a survivor, it is difficult for them not to apply their personal philosophies and solutions to what is happening. It is natural for them to look at a survivor's situation through their eyes and try to help solve the situation in the way that they would solve it in their own personal way. **REMEMBER, YOU ARE UNIQUE. YOU ARE ONLY YOU AND NEED TO HEAL IN YOUR OWN UNIQUE WAY. DO NOT GET SIDETRACKED WITH WHAT OTHER PEOPLE THINK YOU SHOULD BE DOING.**

CHAPTER **24**

THE CEMENT THAT HOLDS THIS ALL TOGETHER

Prayer

Pray, pray, pray. Give your concerns to God and then listen.

> **Do not be anxious about anything, but in everything by prayer and supplication with thanksgiving, let your requests be known to God. And the peace of God, which surpasses all understanding, will guard your hearts and your minds in Christ Jesus. (Philippians 4:6–7)**

> Truly, truly I say to you, whatever you ask of the Father in my name, He will give it to you. **Ask, and you will receive, that your joy may be full. (John 16:23–24)**

On the day I called, you answered me; my strength of soul you increased. **(Psalm 138:3)**

In the day of my trouble, I call upon you, for you answer me. **(Psalm 86:7)**

Seek the Lord and His strength; seek His presence continually! (Psalm 105:4)

EPILOGUE

I hope and pray that you have been supplied with what you need to deal with your grief and heal. I have done my job if you have a new life that has purpose and is meaningful and fulfilled.

Remember:

- Pray your survivor's prayer.
- Put your prayer into practice.
- No big miracles, just steps at a time.
- You are unique. You will heal in your own individual way.
- Your abnormal thoughts and actions at this time are normal, so you are okay where you are right now.
- Talking about your status and expressing how you feel is especially important to help you heal.
- Always keep your self-worth (the importance God puts on you and your life) in the forefront of your mind.
- Know that God has an eternal plan for your life and all other things. That He allows all things to happen for His purposes. His scripture confirms what happens is to glorify Him or what happens results in good.
- To heal, you must be SMART and live SMART:
    S—Serve others
    M—a positive Mental attitude of thankfulness
    A—Activities in a loving and caring environment
    R—Relationships strengthened
    T—Time

May God bless your healing and provide you a meaningful and fulfilled life.

Dear Lord,

I pray this prayer to you asking for
help in my special time of need.

Lord, help me have a **MENTAL ATTITUDE**
of **FAITH** and **TRUST** in you and your
promises that will give me **HOPE** in my life.

I pray that you will help me have a
THANKFUL ATTITUDE about the things
that have happened in my life and that will
happen to me in the future; knowing that
you promised that everything happens for
GOOD IN YOUR ETERNAL PLAN.

Help me understand and accept that the
loss of my loved one creates a **PRIOR LIFE**
about which I never want to forget about, my
love for _____ and the good times; but,
it also creates a **NEW LIFE** that I must live.
Help me understand what changes I must
do to have a **MEANINGFUL NEW LIFE.**

Your word tells me to share each other's
burdens and I want to **SERVE** and help
others. Please help me find ways to serve;
bring people into my life that I can help.
Help me to use the experience of my
loss to help other grieving people.

Lord, I know that **RELATIONSHIPS**
are important for me to recover from
this loss. Please bring people into my
life to fellowship with. Help me find

bible studies and activities where I can
build loving and caring relationships.

Give me strength Lord and lead me into
ACTIVITIES that will help me change
and grow in my new life, always keeping in
mind that my activities are to glorify you.

Please help me to understand that
I must give myself **TIME** to deal
with my human emotions and to
learn how to deal with my loss.

Help me to be patient with
everyone and everything.

Make me more like Jesus in
whose name I pray.

AMEN.

ABOUT THE AUTHOR

The author's faith in his Christian beliefs was sorely tested by the surprise loss of his wife of fifty-two years, Joyce. As he read and studied more and more books on grief and attended grief-help meetings, he could not find any source that seemed to provide everything a survivor needs to know about the grief healing process and struggled to find answers to some major spiritual questions.

His passion is to provide this complete grief handbook on how to heal. Also included are some concepts and answers to questions which he has not found in any other publications.

Unable to find a grief program he felt was comprehensive enough, he designed and conducted an eight-week program for his church and other help programs for the last seven years.

Mr. Thompson has a legal and accounting background which he utilized in providing total financial and estate planning to professional and family-owned businesses over his fifty-year career.

He has four children, nine grandchildren, nine great-grandchildren and remarried five years ago.

CPSIA information can be obtained
at www.ICGtesting.com
Printed in the USA
LVHW010906100222
710101LV00001B/2